Gaslighting & Narcissistic Manipulation: Shining the Light and Reclaiming Your Fire

Navigate through the Shadows of Doubt, Rebuild Your Self-Esteem, and Emerge Empowered in Months—Without Walking Alone

Nicholas Bright

Legal Notice

This book is subject to copyright protection and should only be used for personal use. Furthermore, it should not be shared with any other individual or persons for any purpose other than that for which it was initially intended. It is strictly prohibited to amend, reproduce, distribute, utilize, quote, or paraphrase any part of the content within this publication without prior authorization from the writer or publisher. Any violation of these regulations may result in legal action against those who have breached them.

Disclaimer Notice

The presented work is strictly informational and should not be interpreted as an offer to buy or sell any form of security, instrument, or investment vehicle. Furthermore, the information contained herein should not be taken as a medical, legal, tax, accounting or investment recommendation given by the author(s) or any affiliated company, employees, or paid contributors. In other words, the information is presented without considering individual preferences for specific investments in terms of risk parameters. It is general information that does not account for a person's lifestyle and financial objectives. It is important to note that no tailored advice will be provided based on the given information.

Table of Contents

CHAPTER 3: SPEAKING YOUR TRUTH: MASTERING COMMUNICATION AND ASSERTIVENESS

CHAPTER 4: THE HEALING CORE: EMOTIONAL AND PSYCHOLOGICAL SELF-CARE

CHAPTER 5: TRUST REBUILT: FOSTERING INNER CONFIDENCE AND HEALTHY RELATIONSHIPS 68

CHAPTER 6: VISION OF THE FUTURE: SETTING GOALS FOR PERSONAL AND EMOTIONAL LIBERATION 79

CHAPTER 7: THROUGH THE NARCISSIST'S LENS: DECIPHERING THE MIND OF THE MANIPULATOR

Welcome to the

Ideas Worth Sharing

Series

My name is Nicholas Bright, and I've spent nearly two decades working as a Psychologist specializing in Behavioural Neuroscience and Interpersonal Communication in the US, UK, and Australia. Throughout my career, I've encountered countless stories, experiences, and insights that have shaped my understanding of the human mind and interpersonal interactions.

This series is a collaborative effort, bringing together the experience and expertise of myself and my colleagues: Erica May, Jeff Sharpe, Camila Alvarez, and potentially new faces in the future! We've chosen to write under pen names to respect everyone's privacy and keep the spotlight on the valuable content we offer rather than us as individuals. This decision allows us to freely share our knowledge without the distractions that often come with the limelight. We stand by the authenticity and credibility of the content shared here—our professional integrity remains at the forefront of this series.

We are deeply passionate about our field, and our primary goal is to equip you with practical, research-backed insights that you can implement in your everyday life. Each chapter is designed to inspire and help you better understand yourself and those around you.

We invite you to engage actively with the material: take notes, discuss the ideas with friends and family, and, most importantly, apply the lessons in your daily routine.

1. **Read;** understand what can be done to improve
2. **Reflect;** appreciate your feelings and their origins
3. **Remember;** put your learning into action

Thank you for embarking on this journey of knowledge and growth with us,

Nick

Want to Win Free Books?

Join Our Newsletter!

In this series, we appreciate that someone may find many different books helpful. I certainly know that when discussing sensitive topics like, for example, divorce, we can end up working on grief, anxiety, self-confidence, cognitive dissonance, and lots more. When we encounter a major challenge in life, it is rarely due to one small problem but rather a concoction of our experiences, outlooks, and actions; it's often a deep-rooted issue with many different things we need to uncover and support. We are complicated beings, and we must recognize this. As such, I would love to invite you all to join our newsletter.

In this, I aim to write articles of interest, including excerpts from various books in the series, as well as **vouchers**, **discounts**, and **giveaways**—and of course, no gimmicks or catches. I harbor a deep loathing of companies that offer seemingly amazing deals, only to charge you vast amounts in hidden fees! I vowed to never fall into that trap myself, and any offers I make are designed to be of true benefit and help. If you win a book in a giveaway, I want you to read it with a smile.

Join our newsletter and discover the additional value we can add to your life's curriculum!

Join us at: **www.IdeasWorthSharingSeries.com/newsletter**

See you on the inside!

About the Author: Dr. Nicholas Bright

Dr Nicholas Bright, a highly esteemed Clinical Psychologist based in the vibrant city of New York, is devoted to preventing and treating mental health problems. Nicholas earned his Clinical Psychology degree from Syracuse University, nestled in the heart of New York State. His practice is centred around mindfulness-based therapies, humanistic approaches, and positive psychology principles, enabling individuals to discover their potential and build emotional and psychological resilience.

He has maintained professional ties and a personal friendship with Erica May since their university years. Together, in the Ideas Worth Sharing series, they aim to extend their therapeutic expertise beyond their clinical settings through a series of books on critical psychological topics. This series will delve into various mental health themes, offering comprehensive advice on integrating emotional balance and humanistic practices into everyday life and techniques for fostering positive mental health.

By sharing practical examples and insights from his clinical work, Nick intends to make evidence-based psychological concepts accessible to the general public. His ultimate goal is to empower individuals with the knowledge and tools to manage their mental health effectively, enhance overall well-being, and build resilience.

Preface

"The privilege of a lifetime is to become

who you truly are."

C.G. Jung

In the intricate dance of life, we often find ourselves swaying to the tunes not of our choosing, especially within the shadows of manipulative relationships. This book is a beacon for those who've been trapped by the fog of gaslighting, often orchestrated by those with narcissistic tendencies. Its purpose reaches beyond simple enlightenment; it endeavors to untangle the complex web of emotions, rebuild the crumbled pillars of self-esteem, and light the path toward a stronger, empowered self. My decision to pen these lines was inspired by a culmination of years spent in the counseling chair, witnessing first-hand the silent torment of individuals struggling to reclaim their reality from the clutches of manipulation.

Among the many sources of inspiration, Carl Jung's profound works, advocating for the individuation process and embracing one's true self, have significantly shaped the foundations of this book. The encouragement and support from my dedicated team at Ideas Worth Sharing and my family, who has lovingly stood by my side, have been instrumental in bringing this book to fruition.

As you turn these pages, I extend my deepest gratitude for allowing me the opportunity to share this journey with you. Your decision to explore this book is a courageous step towards healing and rediscovering the essence of who you are beyond the shadows of doubt and manipulation. This book is designed for individuals who've felt the sting of gaslighting, wrestled with the erosion of their reality, and are ready to embark on a quest for clarity, understanding, and empowerment.

A psychology background is optional to understand the content herein. The material is presented in accessible language, aiming to engage, enlighten, and encourage practical application through every step of recovery. Whether you're at the beginning of your journey to reclaim your sense of self or further along yet seeking deeper understanding and validation, this guide is your companion, illuminating the path forward.

Thank you for investing your time and trust in these words. I invite you to continue reading to reach the end and discover the solutions you've been seeking. Let's break the gaslight, embrace the light of truth, and reclaim your fire.

Introduction

In a world that grows increasingly complex by the day, the intricacies of human relationships often present challenges that can deeply impact our mental health and well-being. Among these challenges, the subtle yet profound effects of manipulative behaviors stand out as particularly destructive, affecting countless individuals across the globe. This book seeks to shine a light on one such behavior—gaslighting—a form of psychological manipulation that can undermine an individual's reality, self-confidence, and sense of identity.

At the heart of our exploration is the recognition that knowledge is power. By understanding the mechanisms and impacts of gaslighting, individuals can begin to untangle the web of confusion that such manipulation weaves, finding clarity and strength in the process. This book is not just about identifying the problem; it's about empowering those affected to reclaim control over their lives, guiding them through the darkness of doubt and back into the light of self-assurance and truth.

The journey through these pages is one of hope and healing. It acknowledges the deep scars that gaslighting can leave behind but also celebrates the resilience of the human spirit. Through personal anecdotes, psychological insights, and practical advice, readers are invited to traverse the complicated landscape of emotional manipulation, equipped with the tools they need to emerge stronger on the other side.

Our discussions extend beyond the immediate effects of gaslighting, exploring the broader context of narcissistic manipulation and its place in today's society. By placing gaslighting into this wider perspective, we aim to foster a deeper understanding of the forces that enable such behaviors, equipping readers with a more nuanced view of their interpersonal relationships and the societal structures that shape them.

Central to this narrative is the theme of empowerment through self-awareness and action. Each chapter builds upon the last, forming a roadmap for those seeking to overcome the shadows of manipulation. The emphasis here is on practical strategies—setting boundaries, nurturing self-esteem, and building healthy relationships—that can be implemented daily, laying the groundwork for lasting change.

Acknowledging the diversity of experiences with gaslighting, this book offers a range of perspectives and solutions, understanding that what works for one person may not work for another. It is a testament to the complexity of human relationships and the individualistic nature of healing and growth. Readers are encouraged to approach these strategies with an open mind, adapting them to their unique situations and needs.

Importantly, this book also addresses the role of supporters—friends, family, and allies of those experiencing gaslighting. It underscores the importance of a supportive network, offering guidance on providing meaningful help without becoming overwhelmed. This aspect of the book highlights the communal nature of healing, suggesting that overcoming gaslighting is not just an individual journey but a collective endeavor.

The path to recovery from manipulation is often a labyrinthine one, fraught with challenges and setbacks. This book seeks to be a constant companion through that labyrinth, offering reassurance and guidance at every twist and turn. It acknowledges the non-linear nature of healing, celebrating small victories while providing support through the setbacks, with the ultimate goal of guiding readers toward a place of self-efficacy and peace.

Furthermore, this book outlines the limitations of battling gaslighting alone, advocating for professional assistance when necessary. It provides resources and advice on seeking help, emphasizing that reaching out is not a sign of weakness but strength. By doing so, it aims to destigmatize mental health support, framing it as an integral part of the healing process.

This book stands as a manifesto, affirming the inherent rights to mental and emotional freedom, respect, and dignity. It serves as a rallying cry against the subtle and damaging impacts of gaslighting, offering a light for those seeking to rediscover their strength. Within its pages, readers will discover practical tools and profound insights, joining a supportive community of individuals on the path to healing. Together, we envision a future where manipulation no longer dictates the course of our lives.

Chapter 1: The Smoke and Mirrors of Gaslighting

"The only thing more frustrating than slanderers

is those foolish enough to listen to them."

Criss Jami

Unmasking the Illusion

Gaslighting, a term that has gained prominence in recent discussions surrounding relationships, especially those with a narcissistic partner, is far more than just a buzzword. It's a ruthless manipulation tactic used to sow seeds of doubt in people's minds, making them question their reality, memory, and sanity. This chapter aims to dissect the anatomy of gaslighting, helping you recognize its presence in various contexts and understand its profound impact on your sense of self.

Narcissistic relationships, characterized by an imbalance of power and a profound lack of empathy, are fertile ground for gaslighting. This form of psychological manipulation is wielded like a weapon, aiming not just to confuse but to control. It leaves victims grappling with a distorted self-image and a pervading sense of self-doubt. **Understanding the signs and distinguishing between manipulative tactics and healthy relationship behaviors is the first step to reclaiming your mental space.**

Identifying gaslighting involves recognizing the subtle ways in which reality is distorted by a partner to erode your confidence. This could manifest as denying events ever occurred, trivializing your feelings, or shifting blame to you for their actions. The constant questioning of your reality leads to a deep sense of insecurity, impacting your mental well-being and your emotional stability profoundly. **The aim here is to arm you with the ability to discern these manipulative tactics and differentiate them from genuine, respectful interactions.**

The erosion of self-esteem is a gradual process, where constant doubt seeds grow into towering trees of insecurity. Recognizing this pattern is crucial as it highlights how persistent exposure to narcissistic gaslighting affects one's mental health. Victims often find themselves in a perpetual state of second-guessing, their confidence chipped away by the relentless questioning of their perceptions and decisions.

Acknowledging the impact of narcissistic manipulation on mental well-being is a pivotal portion of this journey toward healing. Understanding that the feelings of confusion, isolation, and self-doubt are not reflections of reality but instead weapons wielded to maintain control is empowering. It begins the process of mental liberation, where recognizing the problem is inherently part of the solution.

Empowerment in this context is about more than just recognizing and naming the problem; it's about actively engaging in strategies to reclaim your sense of self. This involves setting healthy boundaries, fostering relationships based on mutual respect, and cultivating an environment conducive to healing. Practical tools and strategies offered throughout this discussion are designed to illuminate the path from gaslighting's shadows and ensure you're walking it as confidently as possible.

As we navigate this chapter, remember that the journey out of the maze of gaslighting is as much about rediscovering who you are as it is about escaping the manipulation. This is a journey towards regaining trust in your perceptions, building a robust sense of self, and feeling confident in navigating future interactions. The goal is not just to escape the fog but to emerge from it, knowing that someone else's smoke and mirrors can never extinguish your fire.

Gaslighting is a manipulative tactic used by individuals, particularly those with narcissistic tendencies, to distort their victim's reality and control their perception of themselves. It is a form of psychological manipulation that gradually erodes the victim's self-esteem, making them doubt their thoughts, feelings, and experiences. Gaslighting can occur in various contexts, such as personal relationships, workplaces, and societal structures. Regardless of the context, the impact on the victim's sense of reality is profound.

In personal relationships, gaslighting can lead to a pervasive sense of self-doubt and a warped self-image. The constant manipulation by the gaslighter, intentionally or unintentionally, causes the victim to question their thoughts, emotions, and memories. They may feel confused and disoriented as their sense of reality is constantly undermined. Gaslighting tactics can include denying the victim's experiences, manipulating their emotions, distorting facts, and even outright lying. The aim is to gain power and control over the victim by making them depend on the gaslighter for validation and guidance.

In workplace settings, gaslighting can be equally damaging. Employers or colleagues may use manipulative tactics to undermine employees' confidence, skills, or intelligence. This can include taking credit for their work, belittling their achievements, or spreading rumors to damage their reputation. Gaslighting in the workplace can have severe consequences for the victim's professional growth and mental well-being, leading to anxiety, depression, and even post-traumatic stress disorder.

On a societal level, gaslighting can manifest through systemic structures that perpetuate inequality and marginalization. Members of marginalized communities, such as people of color, women, and LGBTQ+ individuals, may be subjected to gaslighting that denies their experiences of discrimination and oppression. This further reinforces power imbalances and silences those who are already marginalized, making it difficult for them to challenge these unjust systems.

Gaslighting, in all its forms, chips away at the victim's sense of self. It gradually erodes their self-esteem and confidence, making them question their reality and worth. They may blame themselves for the gaslighter's behavior, believing they are the problem. This constant manipulation and self-doubt can have severe consequences on the victim's mental well-being and emotional stability. They may experience symptoms of anxiety and depression, struggle with trust and relationships, and have difficulty asserting their own needs and boundaries.

Gaslighting is a form of emotional abuse that leaves its victims feeling trapped and powerless. However, awareness and understanding of gaslighting can help individuals recognize when they are being manipulated and take steps to protect their mental well-being. In the following sections, we will explore healthy behaviors and manipulative tactics in relationships and delve deeper into the gradual erosion of self-esteem caused by narcissistic manipulation. By understanding the dynamics of gaslighting and its impact on our sense of reality, we can reclaim our power and rebuild our self-esteem.

Distinguishing Healthy Behaviors from Manipulative Tactics

Gaslighting is a manipulative tactic used by narcissists to undermine their victim's sense of reality and control them. However, it can be difficult to distinguish between healthy behaviors and manipulative tactics in relationships, especially when you are entangled in the web of gaslighting. In this part, we will explore the key differences between the two, helping you gain clarity and empowering you to identify when you are being manipulated.

One important distinction to keep in mind is that healthy behaviors in relationships are centered around trust, respect, and open communication. Partners in healthy relationships support each other's individuality, validate each other's emotions, and work together to resolve conflicts. They create a safe space for vulnerability and growth. On the other hand, manipulative tactics, such as gaslighting, are characterized by control, deceit, and power imbalance.

Gaslighting often involves the narcissist manipulating the victim's perception of reality, causing them to doubt their own experiences and question their sanity. This can take the form of denying or minimizing the victim's feelings, experiences, or memories, leading to confusion and self-doubt. The gaslighter may also use tactics like blame-shifting, shifting responsibility for their actions onto the victim, or constantly changing the narrative to confuse and disorient them.

Another key difference is that healthy behaviors promote mutual growth and empowerment, while manipulative tactics seek to maintain control and power over the victim. In healthy relationships, partners should encourage personal and professional development, celebrate each other's achievements, and provide support during challenges. They should be equals, respecting each other's autonomy and boundaries. In contrast, gaslighting seeks to diminish the victim's self-worth and independence, making them reliant on the narcissist's validation and approval.

Understanding these differences allows you to recognize when you are being gaslit and take steps to protect yourself. It is important to trust your instincts and pay attention to any inconsistencies or discrepancies in the narcissist's behavior. Remember that gaslighting is a form of manipulation and is not your fault. You deserve to be in a healthy and respectful relationship.

In the next part, we will delve deeper into the gradual erosion of self-esteem caused by narcissistic manipulation and its effects on mental well-being. We will explore the long-term impact of gaslighting and discuss strategies for reclaiming your self-esteem and rebuilding your sense of self. By gaining a deeper understanding of the effects of gaslighting, you will be better equipped to navigate through the shadows of doubt and emerge empowered.

Gaslighting is a manipulative tactic often used by narcissists to control and dominate their victims. One of the most damaging effects of gaslighting is the gradual erosion of the victim's self-esteem. Through a series of subtle or overt manipulations, the narcissist chips away at the victim's confidence, leaving them questioning their reality and feeling confused.

Over time, the constant invalidation and gaslighting from the narcissist can lead to a distorted self-image and a deep sense of insecurity. The victim may start to doubt their thoughts, feelings, and perceptions, wondering if they can trust their judgment. This constant self-doubt can be incredibly destabilizing and impact their mental well-being and emotional stability.

Gaslighting often involves the narcissist denying or minimizing the experiences and emotions of the victim. They might claim that the victim is overreacting, being too sensitive, or even accusing them of making things up. This constant invalidation makes the victim question their reality and wonder if they are the ones to blame for the dysfunction in the relationship.

As the gaslighting continues, the victim may become increasingly dependent on the narcissist for validation and validation. The narcissist may use this dependence to manipulate further and control the victim, making it even harder for them to break free from the cycle of gaslighting.

The gradual erosion of self-esteem caused by gaslighting can have long-lasting effects on the victim's mental health and overall well-being. They may become plagued by self-doubt and constantly question their worth and value. This can lead to feelings of depression, anxiety, and a loss of self-identity.

Recognizing the signs of gaslighting and acknowledging the impact it has on self-esteem is an essential step toward healing. By understanding that the gaslighting is not their fault and that they are not alone in their experiences, victims can start to rebuild their self-esteem and take back their power.

The following section will explore the difference between healthy behaviors and relationship manipulative tactics. By understanding what constitutes healthy behavior, victims can begin to identify the red flags of gaslighting and take steps toward breaking free from the cycle of manipulation.

As you reflect on the subtle yet powerful dynamics of gaslighting, it becomes evident that the erosion of your self-esteem in narcissistic relationships is a slow and insidious process. The blurred lines between reality and manipulation can leave you grappling with self-doubt and a distorted self-image. However, understanding the distinction between healthy behaviors and manipulative tactics is the first step toward reclaiming your sense of self. By recognizing the red flags of gaslighting and acknowledging its impact on your mental well-being, you pave the way for healing and growth.

Remember that regaining your self-worth is a journey, not a destination. It requires patience, self-compassion, and a commitment to your well-being. By learning to trust your instincts and setting boundaries that honor your worth, you can begin to unravel the tangled web of manipulation and rebuild your self-esteem. Embrace the power within you to navigate through the shadows of doubt and emerge stronger on the other side.

In the chapters ahead, you will uncover practical strategies to reclaim your fire, cultivate a resilient mindset, and forge healthy relationships grounded in mutual respect and authenticity. You are not alone in this journey; with each step you take toward self-discovery and empowerment, remember that you hold the key to unlocking your true potential. Through perseverance and dedication, you can break free from the chains of gaslighting and become a brighter, more authentic version of yourself.

Chapter 2: Illuminating the Signs: Breaking Free from the Gaslighter's Grip

"Gaslighting is the systematic attempt by one person

to erode another's reality."

Robin Stern

Piercing Through the Veil of Deception

Recognizing the signs of gaslighting is the equivalent of the first ray of dawn breaking through the darkest night. It heralds the beginning of awareness and the critical first step on your journey towards breaking free from the tight grip of a toxic relationship. Gaslighting, an insidious form of manipulation often wielded by narcissistic individuals, can shatter your self-esteem, alter your sense of reality, and leave you shadowed by doubt. You understand and identify the tactics employed by gaslighters, such as denial, minimization, and manipulation of facts, like arming yourself with the light to navigate through the fog of deception.

Denial, minimization, and manipulating facts are the cornerstones of a gaslighter's arsenal. Denial serves as their shield, outright refusing to acknowledge your reality, thereby questioning its existence. Minimization acts as a dismissive wave, trivializing your emotions and experiences as though they were mere specks of dust, unworthy of notice. Lastly, manipulating facts twists and turns your memory and perception, leaving you questioning the ground beneath your feet. Recognizing these tactics not only unveils the pattern of abuse but also begins to loosen the gaslighter's hold on your reality.

Empowerment begins with **self-reflection**. It's about turning the lens inward and asking yourself the hard questions. Are your feelings and memories constantly dismissed? Do you find yourself questioning your judgments more often than not? Reflecting on these questions, documenting interactions, or keeping a journal can illuminate patterns that, while previously unnoticed, now stand stark against the backdrop of your awareness. This step is not about finding immediate answers but about fostering an environment where you can begin to trust yourself again.

Stepping Back to See the Full Picture

The **importance of early recognition** cannot be overstated. Like a disease, gaslighting can quietly proliferate throughout your psyche, causing damage that becomes harder to heal over time. Recognizing the signs early on, trusting those gut feelings that something isn't right, and paying heed to the red flags can prevent further psychological erosion. Early intervention might mean seeking support from friends, family, or professionals and setting healthy boundaries to safeguard your emotional well-being.

Lighting Your Path Forward

A Step-by-Step Process to Clarity

Step 1: Grasp the Tactics. Allocate time daily to educating yourself on denial, minimization, and fact manipulation. Sight specific examples from your own experiences to connect theory with reality. It shouldn't take more than 30 minutes of reflection each day over a week to start seeing patterns.

Step 2: Initiate Self-Reflection. Dedicate a consistent part of your day, perhaps during a morning routine or right before bed, to journal or consider interactions through a critical lens. Ask yourself pointed questions about your feelings and the validation thereof in your relationships. Approximately 15-20 minutes a day should suffice to instigate a habit of reflection.

Step 3: Recognize and React. As you identify the signs, trust in yourself, and your instincts should reemerge. Allow yourself the space to listen to these feelings and prepare for action. Seeking external support or setting boundaries might initially feel daunting, so give yourself grace during this time. Aim to identify one or two trusted individuals for support or one boundary to assert within a month of starting this process.

Step 4: Resource Gathering. Research and compile a list of helpful books, articles, podcasts, and support groups for a week. Documenting contact information for relevant helplines or organizations can also provide a safety net of resources. This list should continuously evolve as you progress on your journey.

Success in this process is measured not by a radical transformation overnight but by the incremental awakening of your agency. It's about reclaiming your reality, bit by bit, and breaking free from the cycle of gaslighting. The power lies in knowing you are not alone, and reclaiming your fire isn't just possible—it's within reach.

Your journey against gaslighting is unique, and while the path may be fraught with challenges, understanding these manipulation tactics, engaging in introspection, recognizing signs early, and leveraging resources forge a path toward healing and empowerment. As you turn each page of this chapter, remember that it's not just about breaking free—it's about becoming stronger, more resilient, and completely empowered on the other side.

Recognizing the signs of gaslighting is the first step towards reclaiming your power in a toxic relationship. Gaslighting is a form of emotional manipulation where the abuser undermines the victim's reality, causing them to doubt their perceptions, memories, and sanity. By understanding the tactics used in gaslighting, such as denial, minimization, blame-shifting, and manipulation of facts, individuals can gain the knowledge and tools necessary to break free from the gaslighter's grip.

One of the main tactics used in gaslighting is denial. Gaslighters will flat-out deny that certain events or conversations took place, even when there is clear evidence to the contrary. They will make the victim question their memory and make them doubt their version of events. Another tactic is minimization, where the gaslighter downplays the victim's emotions or experiences, making them feel like their feelings are invalid or overdramatic. They might say things like, "*You're being too sensitive*" or "*It wasn't that big of a deal.*" This constant invalidation erodes the victim's sense of self-worth and can lead to self-doubt.

Gaslighters also engage in blame-shifting, where they shift the responsibility for their actions onto the victim. They might say, "*If only you had done this differently, I wouldn't have had to act that way.*" By blaming the victim, the gaslighter avoids taking responsibility for their behavior. Lastly, gaslighters manipulate facts to suit their narrative. They twist the truth, distort reality, and revise history to make themselves look better, and the victims look unreliable. This manipulation of facts can make it even more difficult for the victim to trust their judgment and can lead to a loss of self-confidence.

Understanding these tactics is crucial for breaking free from the cycle of abuse. By recognizing when these tactics are being used against you, you can start to set boundaries and assert yourself against the gaslighter. You can regain your sense of self and reclaim your power by understanding that the gaslighter's behavior is manipulative and not based on reality.

Recognize the Signs: Unmask the Truth

Understanding the tactics used in gaslighting is the first step toward breaking free from the gaslighter's grip. Recognizing when someone is using denial, minimization, blame-shifting, or manipulation of facts to undermine your reality is essential. By identifying these behaviors, you can begin to trust your judgment and regain control over your life.

In the next part of this chapter, we will delve deeper into self-reflection and learn strategies for identifying if you are experiencing gaslighting. By examining your thoughts, emotions, and interactions, you can uncover the subtle ways gaslighting may affect your life. With this self-awareness, you will be better equipped to address the gaslighter's tactics head-on.

Gaslighting is a form of psychological abuse that can have long-lasting effects on your self-esteem and mental well-being. We want to empower you to recognize the signs early and take action to protect yourself. By shedding light on the tactics of gaslighting, we can begin to dismantle its power and create healthier, more fulfilling relationships.

Continue reading the following section to learn how self-reflection can help you identify if you are experiencing gaslighting and take the necessary steps toward reclaiming your power.

Gaslighting is a tactic used by manipulative individuals to gain power and control over their victims. It is a form of psychological abuse that can be incredibly damaging to one's self-esteem and mental well-being. Recognizing if you are experiencing gaslighting is the first step towards reclaiming your power and breaking free from the toxic cycle.

Self-reflection is a crucial tool in identifying gaslighting. Start by examining your thoughts and feelings. Are you constantly doubting yourself or second-guessing your perceptions? **Do you find yourself apologizing for things that aren't your fault or taking the blame for someone else's actions?** These are all signs that you may be experiencing gaslighting.

Another important aspect of self-reflection is examining the dynamics of your relationship. Is there a pattern of manipulation and control? Does your partner constantly deny or dismiss your feelings and experiences? Gaslighting often involves the perpetrator minimizing or invalidating your emotions, making you question your reality.

It can also be helpful to seek support from trusted friends and family members. Discuss your concerns with them and get their perspective. They may provide insights and validate your experiences, helping you see the gaslighting tactics for what they are.

Educating yourself about gaslighting and the tactics used by gaslighters is another essential step in self-reflection. Understanding the dynamics at play allows you to unravel the web of lies and manipulation. Look for resources such as books, articles, or support groups that can provide information and guidance.

Journaling can be a powerful tool for self-reflection. Take the time to write down your thoughts, feelings, and experiences. This can help you gain clarity and perspective and provide a record of the gaslighting behaviors you have witnessed. Writing down your thoughts and experiences can also remind you of your truth, helping you resist the gaslighter's attempts to manipulate and control you.

Reflecting on your experiences, it's important to remember that gaslighting is not your fault. Gaslighters are skilled at manipulation and experts at twisting the truth to serve their purposes. It is not a reflection of your worth or intelligence. By recognizing the signs of gaslighting and engaging in self-reflection, you take the first step towards breaking free from the gaslighter's grip and reclaiming your power.

The Reflective Gaslighting Awareness Framework

The Reflective Gaslighting Awareness Framework is a valuable tool designed to help individuals identify the signs of gaslighting in their interpersonal relationships. By engaging in a step-by-step self-assessment process, readers can understand the presence and impact of gaslighting behaviors in their lives. This framework provides a structured approach to recognizing and addressing gaslighting dynamics, empowering individuals to reclaim their power and break free from manipulation.

Gaslighting Signs and Reflective Questions

At the core of the Reflective Gaslighting Awareness Framework are the gaslighting signs that individuals should be aware of in their relationships. These signs include constantly questioning one's memory or feelings, shifting blame, trivializing emotions, and portraying oneself as the victim. Each sign is coupled with reflective questions to foster self-reflection and raise awareness of gaslighting behaviors.

The framework encourages a deeper understanding of the gaslighting dynamics at play by prompting individuals to reflect on instances where they felt undermined or questioned by their reality due to a partner's actions or comments. Reflective questions may include: *"Have you ever experienced a situation where your partner denied something they had previously said or done?" "Have you ever felt like your emotions were dismissed or minimized by your partner?" or "Do you often find yourself questioning your memory or intuition because of things your partner has said?"*

Frequency, Intensity, and Scoring System

The Reflective Gaslighting Awareness Framework goes beyond simply identifying gaslighting signs. It also serves as a tool for individuals to assess the frequency and intensity of their experiences with gaslighting. This assessment allows individuals to distinguish between isolated misunderstandings and systematic gaslighting, providing a clearer picture of the overall impact on their well-being.

To facilitate this reflection, the framework introduces a scoring system. Readers are encouraged to rate their experiences against each gaslighting sign on a scale where a higher score indicates a higher susceptibility to gaslighting behaviors. This scoring system allows individuals to quantify their experiences and gain a more objective understanding of the presence and severity of gaslighting in their lives.

Personalized Next Steps and Empowerment

Based on the outcome of the scoring system, the Reflective Gaslighting Awareness Framework guides readers toward personalized next steps. These next steps can range from further observation and self-care strategies to seeking professional support. By providing actionable recommendations, the framework empowers individuals to take control of their situations and make informed decisions about addressing and combating gaslighting.

The Reflective Gaslighting Awareness Framework serves as a pathway to empowerment and healing. By engaging in self-reflection and awareness-building, individuals can begin to dismantle the toxic dynamics of gaslighting and regain their sense of self. This framework offers a starting point for individuals to break free from the psychological harm caused by gaslighting and move towards healthier, more respectful relationships.

Practical Implications and Future Development

The Reflective Gaslighting Awareness Framework has practical implications for individuals striving to navigate and address gaslighting. Providing a structured process for self-assessment equips individuals with the tools and insights needed to take action and reclaim their power.

Furthermore, this framework opens up opportunities for future development and application. As individuals engage with the Reflective Gaslighting Awareness Framework, they may discover additional signs and reflective questions to incorporate into their self-assessment process. This ongoing development can refine the framework and enhance its efficacy in helping individuals recognize and address gaslighting behaviors.

42

Remember Your Power in Recognizing Gaslighting Behaviors

As you reflect on the tactics of gaslighting, remember the power that comes with knowledge. Understanding manipulation techniques like denial, minimization, and shifting blame empowers you to reclaim control in toxic relationships. **By identifying these behaviors, you take the crucial first step towards breaking free from the gaslighter's grip.**

Take Action Through Self-Reflection

Self-reflection is your compass in navigating the shadows of doubt cast by gaslighting. By actively assessing your experiences and emotions, you can uncover the subtle signs of manipulation and regain clarity. Use introspection as a tool to identify gaslighting tactics, address self-doubt, and safeguard your well-being.

Embrace Early Recognition for Self-Preservation

Recognizing gaslighting early on is key to preventing further psychological harm. Trust your instincts and be vigilant for the signs, such as distorted reality and questioning your perceptions. Don't wait for the situation to escalate; by acknowledging the warning signs promptly, you can protect yourself and begin the journey to reclaim your sense of self.

Reclaim Your Voice and Set Boundaries

You have the strength to confront gaslighting behaviors and assert your boundaries. Stand firm in your reality, express your needs clearly, and refuse to be manipulated by the gaslighter's tactics. Remember, self-respect is non-negotiable, and setting boundaries is an act of self-care and empowerment.

Illuminate the Shadows and Step into Empowerment

You are paving the way toward liberation and self-reclamation as you shed light on the gaslighting tactics employed against you. Trust in your ability to recognize manipulation, believe in your worth, and take decisive steps toward breaking free from the cycle of abuse. Embrace your inner strength, for it is the guiding force that leads you out of the darkness and into a life of empowerment and authenticity.

Chapter 3: Speaking Your Truth: Mastering Communication and Assertiveness

"Domination does not hear itself.

Power has no ear for the powerless."

Johann Wolfgang von Goethe

Speak Up, Stand Strong

When navigating the treacherous waters of narcissistic manipulation, the ability to communicate effectively becomes your lifeboat. It's not just about talking more; it's about speaking with intention. **Mastering communication and assertiveness is a defense against gaslighting and** a proactive step toward reclaiming control over your narrative and establishing boundaries that protect your emotional well-being. This expertise allows victims of manipulation to transition from a state of confusion and self-doubt to one of clarity and self-assurance.

At the core of overcoming narcissistic manipulation is the skill to *assert personal truth and communicate needs*. This seems straightforward, yet it is incredibly profound. By articulating your needs and truths, you challenge the distorted reality a gaslighter presents. This is not about confrontation but anchoring yourself so firmly in your reality that attempts to unsettle you are less effective. It's a fundamental step in regaining your sense of self.

Practicing assertive communication techniques to counteract gaslighting is another vital skill. Assertive communication is not aggressive; it's a confident and respectful way of expressing yourself. It involves stating your thoughts and feelings firmly and directly without undermining your rights or those of others. This approach can significantly diminish the power a gaslighter has over your emotions and perceptions, making it a crucial strategy in your recovery toolkit.

Setting and enforcing healthy boundaries is equally important. Boundaries act as emotional guardrails, defining where your space begins and ends and what you will tolerate. A lack of clear boundaries invites further manipulation. Learning to set these boundaries confidently and enforcing them consistently is vital in protecting against emotional manipulation. It signals to the gaslighter that their usual tactics will no longer work on you, forcing them to recognize your autonomy.

However, these skills do not develop overnight. Like any form of mastery, they require practice, patience, and persistence. It's about small, consistent efforts to push back against the gaslighting, to express your needs even when it feels uncomfortable, and to stand firm in your truth, even (and especially) when it's challenged.

The Road to Emotional Mastery

Developing these skills is an act of bravery. It means facing the fear of confrontation and the potential for further manipulation head-on. But the reward—regaining control over your life and narrative—is unparalleled. This chapter serves as a beacon of hope and a practical guide for those ready to embark on this journey.

Empowerment lies in the realization that you are not helpless. By adopting assertive communication, you're taking back the pen that writes your story. It's about changing the dynamics of your interactions with a manipulative individual, often leading to a shift in their behavior or, at the very least, safeguarding your mental health.

Remember, mastering communication and assertiveness is critical to healing and empowerment. It enables you to establish firm boundaries, protect yourself from emotional manipulation, and ultimately, reclaim your fire. Start small, be consistent, and watch as you gradually build a fortress around your emotional well-being, capable of withstanding the challenges you face.

Effective communication is the cornerstone of any healthy relationship. It allows individuals to express their needs, voice their concerns, and establish boundaries. However, when you're facing gaslighting behaviors, expressing yourself can feel like an uphill battle. Gaslighting is a manipulation tactic used by narcissistic individuals to make their victims doubt their reality and sanity. But you can regain control over your narrative by developing skills to assert your truth and communicate your needs.

Assertive communication involves expressing your thoughts, feelings and needs directly yet respectfully. It allows you to stand up for yourself without being aggressive or passive. When faced with gaslighting, assertive communication is crucial in countering the manipulative tactics employed by the narcissist. You regain your power and maintain your mental well-being by clearly stating your truth and advocating for yourself.

To develop skills in assertive communication, start by understanding your own needs, beliefs, and values. Take the time to identify what matters most to you and what boundaries you need to establish. This self-reflection will help you gain confidence in expressing yourself authentically. It's also important to remember that your truth and experiences are valid. Gaslighting can make you doubt yourself, but by reaffirming your reality, you can speak your truth with conviction.

Next, practice expressing yourself assertively in various situations. Start with low-stake scenarios, such as making a request to a coworker or setting a boundary with a friend.

Gradually work up to more challenging conditions, such as confronting a gaslighter. Remember to use "*I*" statements to express your feelings and needs, and avoid blaming or accusing language. Be clear and specific about what you want or need, and be prepared to negotiate compromises if necessary.

In addition to assertive communication, active listening is an essential skill in effective communication. Listening to others without judgment or interruption is crucial in building healthy relationships. It allows you to understand others' perspectives, validate their feelings, and respond compassionately and empathetically.

By developing assertive communication skills and actively listening to others, you can protect yourself from further emotional manipulation and establish healthy boundaries. Speaking your truth and expressing your needs are powerful tools in standing up to gaslighters and reclaiming your sense of self. So, are you ready to take the first step in mastering communication and assertiveness? Let's embark on this empowering journey together.

Effective communication and assertiveness are crucial in standing up to gaslighting behaviors and setting healthy boundaries. Gaslighting is a form of psychological manipulation that undermines a person's sanity and makes them doubt their reality. Narcissists often use it to exert control over their victims. Learning to express needs clearly, assert personal truth, and advocate for oneself helps victims regain control over their narrative and establish firm boundaries.

One important aspect of countering gaslighting is practicing assertive communication techniques. Assertiveness involves expressing oneself honestly and respectfully while advocating for one's needs and boundaries. It allows individuals to communicate their feelings, thoughts, and desires without resorting to passive or aggressive behavior. By practicing assertive communication, individuals can protect themselves from further emotional manipulation.

One technique for assertive communication is using "*I*" statements. Instead of making accusatory or generalizing statements, using "*I*" statements allows individuals to express themselves non-confrontationally. For example, instead of saying, "*You always make me feel insignificant,*" an individual can say, "*I feel insignificant when certain things happen.*" This helps to avoid blame and encourages open dialogue.

Another technique is setting clear boundaries. Establishing and enforcing boundaries is essential in protecting oneself from gaslighting and emotional manipulation. Boundaries help individuals define what is acceptable and what is not in their relationships. Communicating these boundaries clearly and assertively is important. Allowing others to understand and respect them, saying "*no*" when necessary, and standing firm in one's boundaries are crucial in countering gaslighting behaviors.

Active listening is also a key component of assertive communication. Active listening involves hearing what the other person is saying, understanding their perspective, and validating their feelings. It requires focusing on the speaker, avoiding interruptions, and reflecting on what has been said. By actively listening, individuals can foster open, honest communication, building stronger relationships and countering gaslighting.

Finally, practicing self-care is essential in maintaining assertiveness and countering gaslighting. Self-care involves engaging in activities that promote physical, emotional, and mental well-being. It helps individuals establish a strong sense of self-worth and confidence, making asserting one's needs and boundaries easier. Self-care can include exercise, meditation, spending time with loved ones, or engaging in hobbies. Taking care of oneself is not selfish but an essential step in protecting against emotional manipulation.

Individuals can counter gaslighting behaviors and regain control over their narrative by practicing assertive communication techniques, setting clear boundaries, actively listening, and prioritizing self-care. It is important to remember that gaslighting is not a reflection of one's worth or sanity but rather a manipulation tactic used by others. By developing strong communication and assertiveness skills, victims can protect themselves from further emotional harm and establish healthy relationships based on trust and respect.

Set and Enforce Healthy Boundaries to Protect Against Emotional Manipulation

Now that you have developed the skills to assert your truth and communicate your needs clearly, it is time to focus on setting and enforcing healthy boundaries. Boundaries act as a protective shield, ensuring that your emotional well-being remains intact while deterring emotional manipulation. Establishing firm boundaries allows you to gain control over your narrative and set the tone for respectful and fulfilling relationships.

Healthy boundaries are essential for protecting yourself against emotional manipulation. They serve as a clear line that separates your needs, values, and limits from those of others. You establish a framework that fosters mutual respect and consideration by defining acceptable and unacceptable behavior. When setting boundaries, consider your values and emotional well-being, and be prepared to communicate them to others assertively.

Recognize Your Worth and Value

One of the first steps in setting healthy boundaries is recognizing your worth and value. Understand that you have the right to be treated with respect and dignity. Acknowledge your inherent worthiness and the importance of your needs and feelings. This recognition will form the foundation of your ability to establish and enforce boundaries.

Be Clear and Specific in Your Communication

When establishing boundaries, it is crucial to be clear and specific in your communication. Clearly state what behavior is acceptable and what is not, leaving no room for misinterpretation. Use "*I*" statements to express your feelings and needs, for example, "*I feel uncomfortable when you speak to me in a condescending tone. I would appreciate it if you could communicate with me respectfully.*" By expressing your needs directly and assertively, you establish clear expectations for how you expect to be treated.

Practice Self-Advocacy

Setting boundaries requires self-advocacy. This means speaking up for yourself, expressing your needs, and asserting your rights. Remember, you can assert your needs, ask for what you want, and refuse what you don't want. Practice expressing your boundaries assertively but respectfully, making it clear that your needs are important and deserve to be honored.

Enforce Your Boundaries

Boundaries are only effective if they are followed and respected. It is crucial to enforce your boundaries consistently to protect yourself from emotional manipulation. Communicate the consequences of crossing your boundaries and be willing to follow through on them if necessary. This might involve setting limits on your time with someone or ending a relationship if the boundaries are consistently violated. Remember, you control your well-being, and enforcing boundaries is a way to maintain your emotional health.

Seek Support and Guidance

Setting and enforcing boundaries can be challenging, especially if you have been subjected to emotional manipulation for a long time. Seek support from trusted friends, family members, or a therapist who can provide guidance and encouragement. Surround yourself with people who respect and support your boundaries, which will reinforce the importance of maintaining them.

Practice Self-Care

Maintaining healthy boundaries requires self-care. Take time for yourself to relax, rejuvenate, and reflect. Engage in activities that bring you joy and fulfillment. Prioritize your well-being and honor your physical, emotional, and mental needs. By taking care of yourself, you reinforce the importance of your boundaries and send a clear message that you value and respect yourself.

Remember, setting and enforcing healthy boundaries is not a one-time task but an ongoing process. As you navigate life and encounter different situations, you may need to reassess and adjust your boundaries accordingly. Be flexible yet firm in upholding your boundaries, and continue to practice assertive communication to protect yourself from emotional manipulation. With time and practice, you will become an expert at setting and enforcing healthy boundaries, empowering yourself to reclaim your fire and live on your terms.

Effective communication and assertiveness are the bedrock of countering gaslighting tactics and safeguarding yourself from emotional manipulation. **Developing the skills to speak your truth clearly and assert your needs is key to regaining control over your narrative**. Remember, your voice matters, and expressing it assertively is your right. **You can confidently defend your reality against gaslighting attempts by practicing assertive communication techniques**. It empowers you to stand firm in your truth, making it harder for manipulators to distort your perception.

Setting and enforcing healthy boundaries form a shield against emotional manipulation. It signals to others what you will and won't accept, creating a protective barrier around your well-being. Boundaries establish the rules of engagement in your relationships, ensuring that you are respected and valued for who you are. Remember, your boundaries are non-negotiable, and enforcing them is an act of self-care and self-respect.

In the face of gaslighting, communicating assertively and setting boundaries are acts of reclaiming your power. You have the strength to navigate through manipulative tactics and emerge stronger. As you continue this journey, remember that your truth is valid, your needs matter, and your boundaries are essential for your emotional well-being.

Empower yourself by honoring your truth and standing firm in your boundaries.

Chapter 4: The Healing Core: Emotional and Psychological Self-Care

"To doubt everything or to believe everything are two

equally convenient solutions; both dispense

with the necessity of reflection."

Henri Poincaré

Rediscover Your Inner Sanctuary: A Practical Guide to Emotional and Psychological Self-Care

The aftermath of gaslighting leaves many scars, invisible yet profound. It's a journey that requires patience, understanding, and a compassionate approach to self-healing. This path, often bumpy and uncertain, demands a toolkit filled not with quick fixes but with sustainable practices that nurture the core of our being. Emotional and psychological self-care stands at the forefront of this healing journey, serving as the bedrock upon which individuals can rebuild a sense of self, restore inner peace, and regain the strength eroded by manipulation.

Self-care—a term often thrown around yet seldom unpacked—entails much more than the occasional indulgence. It's a vital component in the framework of recovery, especially in navigating the complexities of emotional upheaval post-gaslighting. At its essence, self-care involves engaging in activities that foster emotional equilibrium and promote mental well-being. This could range from *mindfulness exercises* and *journaling* to *embracing hobbies* that spark joy, *seeking professional therapy*, and *cultivating supportive, healthy relationships*. The goal is to tailor a self-care regimen that resonates with one's needs, interests, and circumstances, making it a cornerstone of daily life.

Mindfulness, a practice rooted in being present and engaged in the current moment without judgment, offers a robust mechanism for individuals to reclaim control over their thoughts and feelings. Techniques such as *deep breathing, meditation*, and *grounding exercises* serve as anchors, helping to mitigate the tumult of emotions and thoughts that gaslighting survivors often encounter. Additionally, exploring supportive therapies like cognitive-behavioral therapy (CBT) or trauma-focused therapy can provide structured avenues for understanding and processing experiences, promoting a journey toward regaining inner strength.

Embracing *self-compassion* emerges as another critical step in the healing process. The path of recovery from gaslighting is layered with challenges, setbacks, and victories, both big and small. Practicing self-compassion—through self-affirmations, positive self-talk, and granting oneself grace—is pivotal in nurturing one's mental health and fostering patience as the journey unfolds. It's about acknowledging that while the path to recovery may be extended and demanding, each step forward signifies a reclamation of self.

Strategies for Weathering the Storm of Triggers

Navigating through life post-gaslighting involves encountering triggers that can evoke intense emotional responses. Preparing oneself to manage these moments through a range of strategies is crucial. Establishing a calming routine, employing grounding techniques, leaning on supportive individuals, or finding solace in soothing activities are all effective tactics. Recognizing personal triggers and developing customized coping mechanisms can significantly empower an individual, reinforcing a sense of control and resilience.

Navigating the Road to Professional Support

Seeking professional support plays a fundamental role in the healing journey. Identifying therapists or counseling services specializing in trauma, narcissistic abuse, or recovery from gaslighting offers a therapeutic avenue tailored to the unique challenges faced. Moreover, tapping into support groups or organizations dedicated to providing resources for individuals on this path can furnish an additional layer of understanding and community support.

By prioritizing emotional and psychological well-being through self-care practices, mindfulness, supportive therapies, and self-compassion, individuals can navigate the aftereffects of gaslighting with resilience and empowerment. The journey may be fraught with challenges, but reclaiming one's fire and emerging stronger on the other side is within reach with the right tools and support.

Implementing self-care practices and prioritizing emotional well-being are crucial steps in navigating the turmoil of gaslighting. When we experience gaslighting, our emotions are often manipulated and invalidated, leaving us feeling confused, isolated, and doubting our reality. We can reclaim our inner strength and find healing by focusing on self-care and emotional well-being.

One essential self-care practice is to make time for activities that bring you joy and relaxation. Whether taking a walk in nature, practicing yoga, or spending time with loved ones, engaging in activities that nourish your soul can help restore a sense of balance and well-being. It's important to prioritize self-care and make it a non-negotiable part of your daily routine.

Seeking support is another vital aspect of self-care when dealing with gaslighting. Connect with people who understand and validate your experiences - whether it's friends, family, or a support group. Sharing your experiences with others who have gone through similar situations can be immensely healing and empowering. Additionally, consider seeking professional help from a therapist or counselor trained in trauma and abuse. They can provide guidance and support as you navigate the complex emotions and effects of gaslighting.

Practicing mindfulness is also essential in healing from gaslighting. Mindfulness helps us become aware of our thoughts and emotions without judgment, allowing us to cultivate a sense of self-compassion and resilience. By practicing mindfulness meditation or engaging in mindfulness-based activities, we can learn to stay present in the moment, regulate our emotions, and develop a stronger connection to our inner selves.

Incorporating self-care practices, seeking support, and practicing mindfulness are powerful tools for reclaiming our inner strength and healing from gaslighting. By prioritizing our emotional well-being, we can rebuild our sense of self and cultivate resilience. Remember, you are not alone in this journey; there is strength in reclaiming your power. Embrace the healing journey and take the first steps towards healing and empowerment.

Engage in Mindfulness and Supportive Therapies to Rebuild Inner Strength

Rebuilding your inner strength after experiencing gaslighting is a crucial step in the healing process. Mindfulness and supportive therapies can provide the tools and techniques to regain a sense of self and resilience. By actively engaging in these practices, you can cultivate self-awareness, emotional balance, and a deeper understanding of your needs and boundaries.

Mindfulness is bringing focused attention to the present moment without judgment. It is about being fully present in your thoughts, emotions, and physical sensations. Mindfulness can be a powerful tool for healing because it allows you to observe your experiences without getting caught up in them. It enables you to gain clarity, perspective, and self-compassion.

One effective way to incorporate mindfulness into your daily life is through **meditation**. Meditation helps you develop a calm and focused state of mind by quieting the mental chatter and anchoring your awareness in the present moment. You can start with just a few minutes of meditation each day, gradually increasing the duration as you become more comfortable. The goal is not to empty your mind of thoughts but to observe them without judgment and let them pass by.

Another aspect of mindfulness is **body awareness**. Paying attention to your body can help you reconnect with yourself more deeply. Engaging in activities like yoga, tai chi, or simply walking can help you become more aware of your physical sensations, release tension, and cultivate a sense of grounding and stability.

Supportive therapies, such as **talk therapy** or counseling, can provide a safe and confidential space to express your emotions, process your experiences, and gain valuable insights from a trained professional. Therapy can offer guidance, validation, and coping strategies to help you navigate the emotional aftermath of gaslighting.

Group therapy or support groups can also be beneficial as they allow you to connect with others who have experienced similar challenges. This sense of community and understanding can help you realize that you are not alone and provide a supportive network of individuals who can relate to your experiences.

Moreover, **alternative therapies**, such as art therapy, music therapy, or journaling, can provide additional avenues for healing. These creative outlets allow you to express yourself nonverbally and explore your emotions, thoughts, and experiences through different mediums. Engaging in these activities can often lead to powerful insights and serve as a form of self-expression and release.

By engaging in mindfulness and supportive therapies, you actively invest in your healing journey and rebuild your inner strength. These practices offer invaluable tools for self-reflection, emotional regulation, and personal growth. While the healing process may take time and effort, know that you have the power within you to reclaim your sense of self and emerge stronger, more resilient, and more empowered than ever before.

Embrace Self-Compassion and Patience in the Healing Journey

In the journey to heal from gaslighting and reclaim inner strength, embracing self-compassion and patience is crucial. It is important to recognize that healing takes time, and setbacks are a natural part of the process. By practicing self-compassion, we offer ourselves kindness, understanding, and forgiveness, ultimately nurturing our emotional well-being. Additionally, cultivating patience allows us to navigate the highs and lows of recovery without becoming overwhelmed or discouraged.

The Role of Self-Compassion

Self-compassion is treating oneself with the same kindness and understanding we would extend to a close friend. It involves acknowledging and accepting our pain, flaws, and mistakes instead of criticizing or judging ourselves harshly. Self-compassion allows us to create a safe and nurturing environment, fostering healing and self-growth.

By practicing self-compassion, we shift our perspective from self-judgment to self-acceptance. Rather than berating ourselves for falling victim to gaslighting or questioning our decisions, we offer ourselves compassion and understanding. This compassionate stance helps us to build resilience, counter self-doubt, and promote emotional healing.

The Power of Patience

Healing from gaslighting is not linear and often involves setbacks and challenges. Patience plays a vital role in navigating this journey. It helps us surrender to the ebb and flow of emotions rather than resisting or becoming frustrated. When we approach our healing journey patiently, we permit ourselves to take the time and space to heal fully.

By practicing patience, we create a supportive and non-judgmental inner dialogue. We acknowledge that healing does not happen overnight and that setbacks are a natural part of the process. This understanding allows us to keep moving forward, even when progress feels slow or non-existent. Patience helps us cultivate resilience and grit, enabling us to stay committed to our healing journey despite obstacles.

Integrating Self-Compassion and Patience in the Healing Journey

Integrating self-compassion and patience into our healing journey is a conscious and ongoing practice. Here are some strategies to help you embrace these qualities:

1. **Self-Reflection**: Reflect on your experiences, emotions, and behaviors without judgment. Use journaling or meditation to create a safe space for self-exploration and self-compassion.
2. **Self-Care**: Engage in self-care activities that nourish your mind, body, and soul. This can include anything from walking in nature to practicing yoga or engaging in creative outlets like painting or writing.
3. **Support System**: Surround yourself with supportive and understanding individuals who can provide validation and encouragement. Seek out a therapist, support groups, or online communities where you can share your experiences and receive empathy.
4. **Mindfulness**: Practice mindfulness to cultivate self-awareness and non-judgment. By observing your thoughts and feelings without getting caught up in them, you can develop a compassionate and patient stance towards yourself.

5. **Setting Boundaries**: Prioritize setting and enforcing healthy boundaries in your relationships. This allows you to protect yourself from further gaslighting and create a safe space for healing.

Remember, healing is a journey, and embracing self-compassion and patience is essential. By treating yourself with kindness and extending patience to your healing process, you can reclaim your inner strength and emerge from gaslighting with resilience and a newfound sense of self. Embrace the power of self-compassion and patience, and you will pave the way for lasting healing and personal growth.

Moving Forward: Your Healing Path

As you navigate the aftermath of gaslighting, trust that **you have the power within you to reclaim your sense of self** and rebuild the strength that was once tarnished. **Prioritize your emotional well-being** as you embark on this healing journey. Embrace each day with **self-compassion**, understanding that healing is not a linear path—it's a series of small steps forward, sometimes with setbacks, but always with progress. **Practice mindfulness** to ground yourself in the present moment, allowing yourself to feel and process your emotions without judgment.

Take Action: Empower Your Healing

In the days to come, commit to **prioritizing yourself**. Engage in **self-care practices** that nurture your mind, body, and soul. Seek supportive therapies that resonate with you, whether counseling, journaling, or connecting with a trusted friend. Remember, **you have the strength to rise above the shadows of doubt** cast by gaslighting. Your journey to reclaim your fire starts with a single step—one that you are fully capable of taking.

Chapter 5: Trust Rebuilt: Fostering Inner Confidence and Healthy Relationships

"Manipulation is when they blame you for your

reaction to their disrespect."

Unknown

Rebuilding From the Ashes: A Journey Towards Self-Trust and Interpersonal Healing

The aftermath of gaslighting can leave one's sense of reality and self-worth severely eroded. It's akin to waking up in a landscape you once knew, only to find it unrecognizable. This journey, central to "*Breaking the Gaslight: Shining a Light on Narcissistic Manipulation and Reclaiming Your Fire,*" is not merely moving past the experience but **transforming it into a stepping stone for growth**. In this pivotal chapter, we explore practical, actionable steps towards rekindling the sparks of trust in oneself and relationships, critical in the face of gaslighting's cold darkness.

The path toward **rebuilding inner trust is both delicate and profound**. It begins with accepting that the gaslighting wasn't a reflection of your lack of judgment or worth but a deliberate act of manipulation by another. This acceptance isn't an end but a starting point. It's about **cultivating a relationship with oneself rooted in compassion and understanding**, acknowledging that the journey back to self-trust will require patience and enduring commitment.

Self-Trust Illuminated: Navigating Uncertainty with Confidence

Cultivating self-trust and intuition is the first critical step in safeguarding against future manipulation. This involves reflecting **on one's strengths, abilities, and accomplishments**, reinforcing the foundation of self-esteem that gaslighting seeks to undermine. Exercises such as journaling about times when you trusted your intuition and the outcome was positive can be immensely helpful. By doing so, you recognize your inherent worth and capabilities and begin to listen more attentively to your inner voice, which is critical in trusting your instincts in relationships.

Recognizing and fostering healthy relationship dynamics is the following cornerstone. Understanding the traits of healthy relationships like mutual respect, open communication, and trust becomes paramount after gaslighting. It's about setting boundaries and being vigilant against behaviors that feel all too familiar yet harmful. Learning to **seek and build relationships founded on reciprocity and mutual support** is healing and empowering as a protective barrier against future manipulation.

Cultivating a Garden of Support: Nurturing Growth and Self-Worth

Surrounding oneself with **supportive individuals** who affirm your values and encourage your growth is essential. Identifying these individuals—be they friends, family, or support groups—provides a **haven for emotional support and constructive feedback**. This network becomes your echo chamber for positivity and validation, crucial to rebuilding your self-worth and confidence post-gaslighting.

Navigating Stormy Seas: Co-parenting and Maintaining Necessary Contacts

For many, completely severing ties with the gaslighter isn't always possible, especially in cases of co-parenting. The guiding principles are setting firm boundaries, communicating assertively, and prioritizing personal well-being. While navigating this dynamic is challenging, **legal advice or professional counseling** can offer strategies to manage this relationship effectively, ensuring the focus remains on your healing journey and the well-being of any children involved.

Reflective Journey: A Path of Continuous Growth

Finally, the process calls for **ongoing self-reflection** and growth. Regularly checking in with oneself and trusted friends or family for signs of gaslighting or manipulation in relationships is crucial. **Embrace professional help** if the journey seems overwhelming. It's about ensuring that the relationships you cultivate, including the one with yourself, serve your highest good and provide a life rich with mutual respect, love, and understanding.

While not exhaustive, this step-by-step process serves as a guide leading you through the aftermath of gaslighting. It emphasizes the significance of patience, self-love, and resilience. Each step represents a **foundation for reclaiming your inner strength**, demonstrating your fortitude and steadfast dedication to emerging from the shadows of uncertainty empowered and whole. The path to healing and rediscovering your individuality may be challenging, yet it is deeply fulfilling, illuminating a journey toward a more resilient, authentic, and unapologetically genuine self.

In the aftermath of gaslighting, rebuilding trust within oneself and in relationships is vital. Gaslighting erodes our ability to trust our intuition and judgment, leaving us feeling lost and uncertain. But there is hope. By cultivating self-trust and intuition, we can safeguard ourselves against future manipulation and reclaim our inner confidence.

To begin rebuilding trust, it is essential to acknowledge and validate our past experiences. Gaslighting can be a form of emotional abuse, and its effects can linger long after the abusive relationship has ended. Take the time to process these experiences and recognize their impact on your sense of self and trust. By acknowledging the pain and trauma, you can begin the healing process.

Trusting your instincts is another crucial step in rebuilding trust. Gaslighting often makes us doubt ourselves and our perceptions, but deep down, we still can sense when something is off. Start by listening to those gut feelings and learning to trust them again. Your intuition is a powerful tool that guides you towards what suits you.

Alongside cultivating self-trust, it is equally important to foster healthy relationship dynamics. Gaslighting can leave us wary of opening up to others or vulnerable to falling into similar patterns. Take the time to reflect on what healthy relationships look like to you and what you need from them. Establish clear boundaries and communicate openly with the people in your life. Surrounding yourself with individuals who respect and support you is crucial for rebuilding trust.

Perhaps most importantly, practice self-love and self-compassion throughout this journey. Rebuilding trust takes time and patience. It is expected to have setbacks and moments of doubt, but remember that you are worthy of love and respect. Treat yourself with kindness and understanding as you navigate through the healing process.

By cultivating self-trust, recognizing the impact of past traumas, and fostering healthy relationship dynamics, you can rebuild trust in yourself and others. Trust cannot be rebuilt overnight, but with time and dedication, you can emerge stronger and more confident from the shadows of gaslighting. The following section will delve deeper into recognizing and fostering healthy relationship dynamics post-gaslighting.

Recognizing and fostering healthy relationship dynamics after experiencing gaslighting is crucial in rebuilding trust and self-worth. Gaslighting can leave individuals feeling unsure of themselves and hesitant to trust others again. However, by understanding what healthy relationships look like and actively working towards fostering those dynamics, it is possible to create fulfilling and supportive connections.

One key aspect of healthy relationship dynamics is mutual respect and equality. In healthy relationships, both parties value and respect each other's thoughts, opinions, and boundaries. There is a sense of equality where power and decision-making are shared. By recognizing the importance of these qualities, individuals can set clear boundaries and communicate openly about their needs, ensuring that their voices are heard and respected.

Furthermore, fostering healthy relationship dynamics involves effective communication. This means actively listening to each other, validating feelings, and expressing oneself assertively without the need for manipulation or control. Healthy communication allows for honest and open dialogue, resolving conflicts respectfully. By developing these skills, individuals can create an environment where their emotions and perspectives are understood and valued.

Another crucial aspect of healthy relationships is trust. Rebuilding trust after experiencing gaslighting may feel challenging, but it is essential to developing strong bonds. This involves being vulnerable, sharing thoughts and feelings honestly, and believing in the authenticity of the other person's words and actions. Practicing trust-building exercises, such as setting small goals and achieving them together, can help rebuild trust gradually.

Self-awareness and self-care are also vital when fostering healthy relationship dynamics. Understanding one's needs, desires, and limits enables individuals to communicate effectively and establish boundaries. Taking time for self-care through therapy, self-reflection, or engaging in activities that bring joy and fulfillment allows individuals to nurture their emotional well-being and maintain a healthy sense of self.

Finally, surrounding oneself with supportive individuals encouraging growth and self-worth is crucial for fostering healthy relationships. Building a strong support system of friends, family, or even support groups can provide validation, understanding, and the reassurance needed to overcome past trauma and develop healthy relationship patterns. These supportive relationships create a sense of belonging and offer a safe space to share experiences, feelings, and challenges.

Surround Oneself with Supportive Individuals Who Encourage Growth and Self-Worth

Rebuilding trust and self-worth after experiencing gaslighting is not a journey that anyone should have to navigate alone. It is crucial to surround yourself with supportive individuals who understand your experiences, validate your emotions, and encourage personal growth. These individuals can play a vital role in helping you rebuild trust in yourself and others, fostering a sense of belonging, and boosting your self-esteem.

Supportive relationships provide a safe space to share your thoughts and feelings without fear of judgment or manipulation.

Whether it is a close friend, family member, therapist, or support group, having others who believe in you and your experiences can offer a significant source of validation. Hearing others acknowledge the impact of gaslighting and empathizing with your journey can be incredibly healing.

When choosing your support network, be mindful of their intentions and values. Seek out individuals who prioritize your emotional well-being and growth rather than those who enable victimhood or encourage negative patterns. Faithful supporters will lift you, challenge your self-doubts, and remind you of your strengths. They will help you see your worth and provide a solid foundation for rebuilding trust in yourself and others.

Additionally, being part of a supportive community, either online or in-person, can be immensely helpful in your healing process. Connecting with others who have experienced gaslighting can provide a sense of camaraderie and shared understanding. Within these communities, you can ask questions, gain insights, and support others, creating a network that fosters collective healing and empowerment.

Incorporating self-love and self-care practices into your daily life is crucial when rebuilding trust and self-worth. Treat yourself with kindness, compassion, and patience. Engage in activities that bring you joy and provide a sense of grounding. Prioritize your physical and mental well-being, ensuring you get ample rest, eat nourishing foods, and exercise regularly.

One powerful way to enhance your self-worth is to celebrate your achievements, no matter how small.

Acknowledge your progress in rebuilding trust, noting the steps you have taken towards healing. Give yourself credit for your resilience and growth, and let go of any self-blame or shame that lingers from past experiences.

Remember, rebuilding trust and self-worth is an ongoing process that requires time, self-compassion, and patience. Surrounding yourself with supportive individuals who understand your journey, foster growth, and encourage self-worth is essential during this time. By cultivating these relationships and practicing self-love, you can rebuild trust in yourself and others and emerge stronger, more empowered, and ready to foster healthy and fulfilling relationships.

Rebuilding trust in oneself and relationships post-gaslighting is a journey that requires patience, self-compassion, and courage. **Cultivating self-trust** and listening to intuition are vital to safeguarding against future manipulation. By honoring your instincts and valuing your inner voice, you equip yourself with a shield against deception. **Recognizing and fostering healthy relationship dynamics** is essential in moving forward. Nurture relationships that respect boundaries, communicate openly, and uphold mutual support—these pillars of healthy connections. **Surrounding yourself with supportive individuals** who uplift your growth and self-worth is paramount. Seek out those who celebrate your strengths, offer constructive feedback, and stand by you in times of need.

In the aftermath of gaslighting, grappling with doubts and fears is normal. However, **embracing self-compassion** and acknowledging your past traumas are profound steps toward healing. Be gentle with yourself, for the scars left by manipulation may take time to fade. As you navigate the shadows of doubt, remember that your experiences have not diminished your worth. **Practicing self-love** is not a luxury but a necessity. Treat yourself with kindness, forgive your past mistakes, and celebrate your victories, no matter how small. Through these acts of self-care, you reclaim your power and rebuild the trust that was once shattered.

As you walk the path of rebuilding trust and self-worth, remember that you are not alone. **You possess the resilience and strength** to overcome the challenges before you. Trust in your ability to navigate through the complexities of healing. By fostering self-trust, nurturing healthy relationships, and surrounding yourself with a supportive community, you pave the way for a brighter, more authentic future. Stand tall in your journey of reclaiming your fire, for within you lies the power to emerge empowered and resilient.

Chapter 6: Vision of the Future: Setting Goals for Personal and Emotional Liberation

"The greatest challenge in life is discovering who you are.

The second greatest is being happy with what you find."

Auliq Ice

Embrace Your Liberation: Mapping a Path to Emotional Autonomy

After enduring the labyrinth of gaslighting and emerging from the shadows of emotional manipulation, the natural question arises: "*What's next?*" The recovery and reclamation of self after such experiences is challenging and immensely rewarding. This pivotal phase demands a compassionate understanding of one's past pain and a clear vision for the future. **Establishing personal healing and growth goals** is not just a step towards regaining lost agency; it is an act of defiance against the echoes of manipulation, an affirmation of one's autonomy and value.

The process begins by envisioning a life transcending past experiences' turmoil. This requires a sincere effort to **imagine a fulfilling life beyond the shadows of gaslighting**, where one's desires, passions, and aspirations take center stage, untethered from the influence of manipulative forces. It's about drafting a blueprint of a life that resonates with the depths of one's being, a life that is authentically yours. The significance of this phase cannot be overstated—it is the bedrock upon which the edifice of your emotional liberation is built.

Taking **proactive steps towards achieving emotional autonomy and resilience** involves more than mere wishful thinking; it calls for actionable strategies to reinforce one's sense of self and purpose. This might range from setting boundaries that protect your emotional space to engaging in activities that foster self-exploration and growth. Every deliberate action is a brick on the path toward emotional liberation, a signpost that guides you back to yourself.

It is imperative to cultivate environments that nurture your healing journey. Surrounding yourself with supportive networks, seeking professional guidance, and engaging with communities that uplift your spirit are crucial aspects of this process. These pillars provide strength and stability, ensuring that the road to recovery is not walked alone but accompanied by a chorus of understanding and encouragement.

Prioritizing personal growth and well-being is paramount, but it's equally important to recognize that this journey is uniquely yours. It unfolds at your own pace, guided by your internal compass. Therefore, allow yourself the grace to explore, stumble, and rise, knowing that each step forward is a testament to your resilience and determination.

Indeed, setting long-term goals for personal growth after gaslighting is more than a process—it's a proclamation of your rebirth. It's an acknowledgment of the past that shaped you and a determined focus on the future you deserve. By embarking on this voyage, you are not just reclaiming your fire but inviting it to burn brighter than ever, illuminating the path to a life of emotional autonomy, resilience, and unapologetic joy.

The strategies highlighted in this discussion are not merely theoretical concepts; they are lifelines, practical tools designed to empower you to **navigate the shadows of doubt**, rebuild your self-esteem, and emerge empowered. Every step taken is an act of courage, a piece of the puzzle that gradually forms the picture of your new horizon—a horizon defined by emotional liberation and the fulfillment of your deepest aspirations.

The journey towards healing and growth after experiencing gaslighting can feel overwhelming and uncertain. Establishing personal healing and growth goals is essential to reclaiming agency and taking proactive steps toward a brighter future. Setting long-term goals for personal growth is empowering and helps reclaim agency and autonomy. It allows individuals to envision a positive future and take concrete steps toward creating a life aligned with their values and aspirations.

Setting personal healing goals is an important part of the recovery journey. It helps individuals focus their energy and attention on what matters most. Whether rebuilding self-esteem, healing from trauma, or establishing healthy boundaries, setting specific goals provides direction and accountability. These goals can be short-term or long-term, depending on individual needs and priorities. The key is ensuring they are realistic, measurable, and aligned with one's values.

In addition to personal healing goals, setting growth goals is equally important. This involves identifying areas that need improvement or exploration in one's life. It could be developing new skills, pursuing education or career opportunities, nurturing relationships, or exploring personal interests. Growth goals provide a sense of purpose and motivation, encouraging individuals to step out of their comfort zones and embrace new experiences.

Taking proactive steps towards change is crucial in the journey towards emotional liberation. This involves developing a plan of action and implementing strategies that support personal growth and healing goals. It may include seeking therapy or counseling, practicing self-care, engaging in self-reflection and journaling, surrounding oneself with supportive and loving people, and embracing a growth mindset.

The process of setting personal healing and growth goals can be transformative. It gives individuals a sense of agency and control over their lives. It allows them to step out of the shadows of gaslighting and into a future filled with hope and possibility. Through the power of goal-setting, individuals can reclaim their fire, rebuild their self-esteem, and emerge stronger and more empowered than ever before.

As you embark on this journey of personal growth and emotional liberation, remember you are not alone. There is a community of individuals who have experienced similar struggles and have found their way towards healing and empowerment. Together, we can break free from the chains of gaslighting and shine a light on narcissistic manipulation. So, what are you waiting for? Let's take the next step together if you're ready to reclaim your fire and create a life aligned with your values and aspirations.

Envisioning a fulfilling life beyond the shadows of gaslighting is vital in the journey toward personal and emotional liberation. When you have been manipulated and gaslighted, it can feel as though your dreams and aspirations have been stifled or even extinguished. But it is important to remember that your past experiences do not define you. You have the power to create a new future, one that is aligned with your values and filled with joy, purpose, and fulfillment.

As you begin to envision this future, it is important to let go of any self-limiting beliefs that may have been instilled in you through gaslighting. Remember that you are capable, deserving, and worthy of happiness and success. Allow yourself to dream big without fear or hesitation. What would your ideal life look like? What goals would you set for yourself if you knew that failure was not an option?

Take a moment to reflect on these questions. Close your eyes and imagine your future self, free from the shadows of gaslighting. What does this version of yourself look like? How does it feel to have reclaimed your power and autonomy? What dreams and aspirations are you pursuing? Visualize every detail of this life, from your relationships to the career you've built to the hobbies and passions that bring you joy.

Setting goals for personal and emotional growth is essential to this envisioning process. These goals serve as guiding lights, pointing you toward your desired life. They can range from small, everyday goals to more significant, long-term aspirations. Perhaps you want to work on building your self-esteem and self-worth, or maybe you aspire to establish healthier boundaries in your relationships. Write your goals down and commit yourself to prioritizing your growth and well-being.

Remember, these goals are not static. As you evolve and grow, your goals may change as well. Be open to revisiting and revising them as needed. The important thing is to keep moving forward, taking proactive steps towards change and personal liberation.

But setting goals is not enough. It is equally important to take action to achieve them. Break your goals into smaller, manageable steps and create a plan for yourself. What concrete actions can you take daily, week, or month to move closer to your goals? Hold yourself accountable and celebrate each milestone along the way.

Envisioning a future beyond gaslighting is not just wishful thinking—it is about taking ownership of your life and reclaiming your power. You are actively creating the life you deserve by setting goals and taking action. Keep your vision focused, stay committed to your goals, and never forget you can achieve great things. The journey may not always be easy, but the rewards that await you are worth every step.

Framework: The Path to Emotional Autonomy and Resilience

The framework presented here is designed to assist individuals in their journey toward emotional autonomy and resilience after experiencing gaslighting. It is a three-stage process that begins with reflection, moves into goal formulation, and concludes with action planning. Each stage is crucial in empowering individuals to reclaim agency and create a positive future aligned with their values and aspirations.

Reflection: Acknowledging the Impact

In the reflection stage, individuals are encouraged to contemplate their experiences and acknowledge the impact gaslighting has had on their lives. This self-reflection is essential for gaining clarity and understanding and identifying the lessons learned from these challenging experiences.

During this stage, individuals are invited to examine their emotions, thoughts, and behaviors and recognize any patterns or beliefs that may have been influenced by gaslighting. This process of self-discovery is an opportunity to heal past wounds, build self-awareness, and lay a solid foundation for personal growth.

Goal Formulation: Defining the Future

Once individuals have gained clarity through reflection, the next stage involves formulating specific, measurable, achievable, relevant, and time-bound (SMART) goals. These goals are focused on areas critical to recovery and empowerment, such as developing self-trust, cultivating resilience, and establishing healthy boundaries in relationships.

Setting SMART goals gives individuals a clear vision of their desired future and helps them stay motivated throughout their recovery journey. These goals serve as guiding principles, reminding individuals of their inner strength and the changes they wish to make.

Action Planning: Stepping into Empowerment

The final stage of the framework is action planning, where individuals take proactive steps to achieve their goals for emotional autonomy and resilience. This stage involves creating practical strategies and implementing specific actions aligning with the objectives.

Action planning may include engaging in self-care practices, seeking supportive relationships, developing assertiveness skills, practicing positive self-talk, or pursuing therapy or coaching. The focus is on taking small, concrete steps that gradually build momentum and establish new habits and behaviors.

The framework also includes worksheets for goal setting and action planning, which provide individuals with a structured approach to guide them through the process. Along with these tools, the framework offers tips for overcoming obstacles and maintaining motivation, ensuring individuals have the support and resources they need to succeed.

Empowering Change: Taking Control of Your Future

The path to emotional autonomy and resilience is not always easy. Still, with the proper framework and tools, individuals can navigate the shadows of gaslighting and emerge stronger than ever. By engaging in reflection, goal formulation, and action planning, individuals can set the stage for personal growth and create a life aligned with their values and aspirations.

This framework empowers individuals to reclaim agency and take control of their future. It provides a roadmap for healing, growth, and empowerment, helping individuals overcome the effects of gaslighting and build a foundation for a fulfilling life beyond the shadows.

Remember, you are not alone in this journey. Resources and support are available to you as you embark on this path of personal liberation. Utilizing the tools and strategies provided in this framework, you can embrace your true self, reclaim your fire, and create a life of emotional autonomy and resilience.

Embrace Your Journey Towards Liberation

As you reflect on the path charted in this chapter, remember that setting personal goals for growth is not just a mere exercise; it is a declaration of your resilience, a testament to your unwavering spirit, and a profound commitment to your well-being. Envisioning a life beyond the shadows of gaslighting is not a lofty dream but a tangible reality waiting for your embrace. By establishing clear goals for healing and growth, you reclaim the reins of your life that were once manipulated by narcissistic forces.

Imagine the tapestry of your future woven with threads of empowerment, self-love, and genuine joy. Hold onto this vision as you navigate the sometimes rocky terrain of emotional recovery. *The proactive steps you take today, no matter how small, can shape the landscape of your tomorrow.* Each stride towards emotional autonomy and resilience reinforces your inner strength and capacity to overcome past wounds.

Propel Yourself Towards Your Aspirations

As you move forward, let your personal goals remain readily accessible as sources of hope and inspiration. **Envision the person you aspire to become, and let that vision guide your path through moments of doubt and struggle.** Taking proactive steps towards change is not a sign of weakness but a testament to your inner grit and determination. **Embrace the power within you to steer your life towards fulfillment and contentment.**

Prioritize your growth and well-being, nurturing your spirit with the care and attention it deserves. Each day offers a new canvas to paint your aspirations and desires. Your journey toward personal liberation is not a sprint but a marathon, and every step you take brings you closer to the finish line of emotional empowerment. **Trust in your ability to navigate the shadows of doubt, rebuild your self-esteem, and emerge as a guiding light.**

The Road Ahead Beckons with Promise

As you close this chapter, remember that the key to reclaiming your fire lies in your unwavering commitment to personal growth and emotional healing. With each goal you set, each dream you dare to dream, and every action you take toward self-betterment, you inch closer to the future you envision. Embrace the journey ahead with courage and conviction, knowing that you hold the power to shape your destiny.

Stay true to yourself, anchor yourself in your aspirations, and let the fire of resilience within you burn brightly, illuminating a life of freedom, authenticity, and unwavering self-love. The road ahead beckons with promise, and your journey toward personal and emotional liberation is a testament to your strength, resilience, and unyielding spirit.

Chapter 7: Through the Narcissist's Lens: Deciphering the Mind of the Manipulator

"A lie can travel halfway around the world while the

truth is putting on its shoes."

Charles Spurgeon

Unlocking the Narcissist's Mind

Understanding the complex web of narcissistic manipulation requires delving deep into the psychological underpinnings of such behavior. This insight is not merely academic; it holds the key to unlocking patterns of abuse and gaslighting that many find themselves entangled in. At the heart of narcissistic manipulation lies a set of predictable, though deeply entrenched, behaviors and motivations that can be understood and, more importantly, defended against. It's crucial for anyone who finds themselves in the orbit of a narcissist to grasp these concepts not as abstract theories but as tools for personal liberation.

Narcissistic Personality Disorder (NPD) and **covert narcissism** are terms that often come up in discussions about narcissistic abuse. Yet, their clinical definitions and manifestations in everyday life are not always well-understood. NPD is characterized by an inflated sense of self-importance, a deep need for excessive attention and admiration, troubled relationships, and a lack of empathy for others. Covert narcissism, on the other hand, presents as a quieter, more insidious form of narcissism, where the individual displays excessive humility, sensitivity to criticism, and a penchant for playing the victim. Both forms are damaging, but understanding their nuances is critical for recognizing the signs and protecting oneself.

The Mechanics of Gaslighting

Gaslighting, a form of psychological manipulation where the abuser sows seeds of doubt in the victim, making them question their reality, judgment, and sanity, is a favored tool of the narcissist. This technique doesn't just occur in overt, easily identifiable situations. It often happens incrementally, with the narcissist skillfully disorienting their victim's perception of reality over time. The ultimate aim is control and domination. Recognizing this strategy is the first step in disarming it.

Knowledge of its workings empowers the victim to trust their perceptions and judgments again, effectively breaking the cycle of manipulation.

Empowerment Through Education

Education is a shield against further psychological abuse. Understanding the psychological theories behind narcissistic behaviors demystifies the narcissist's actions. It reframes the narrative, allowing victims to see the manipulations for what they are: tactics of control, not reflections of their failings. This shift in perspective is profoundly empowering. It moves individuals from a stance of vulnerability to one of informed strength. With this knowledge, strategies for defense and recovery can be developed, tailored to each unique situation but grounded in a shared understanding of the narcissist's playbook.

The insight from exploring these psychological concepts does more than arm individuals against further harm. It fosters a deeper understanding of self and other relationships that may have been previously affected by narcissistic manipulation. Learning to recognize the red flags of NPD and covert narcissism and understanding the mechanics behind gaslighting equips individuals not only to navigate but also to heal from these experiences.

Empowerment through education means recognizing one's capacity to overcome the challenges posed by narcissistic abuse, trusting in one's ability to rebuild self-esteem, and reasserting control over one's life. This process is not instantaneous. It requires patience, persistence, and, often, support from others who have walked the same path.

The psychological theories behind narcissistic behaviors provide a framework for understanding not just the *what* but the *why* of manipulation. This understanding is crucial for moving beyond the role of victim to emerge as a survivor, empowered and informed. Through education, victims can transform their experience into knowledge, turning what was once a source of pain into a tool for empowerment and protection. By learning to identify and understand the patterns of narcissistic abuse, individuals reclaim their fire, lighting the way forward for themselves and others.

Understanding the psychological theories behind narcissistic behaviors is key to deciphering the mind of a manipulator. By exploring these theories, we can gain valuable insight into the dynamics of abuse and manipulation, particularly when it comes to gaslighting. Gaslighting is a manipulative tactic used by narcissists to distort reality, undermine victims' self-esteem, and gain control over them.

One psychological theory that sheds light on gaslighting is cognitive dissonance. This theory suggests that when individuals encounter information or experiences that contradict their beliefs or self-image, they experience psychological discomfort. This discomfort motivates them to change their beliefs or dismiss the contradicting information. Narcissists exploit this cognitive dissonance in their victims by manipulating their perception of reality and making them doubt their own experiences. Gaslighting is a deliberate tactic used to create confusion and control.

Another theory that helps explain narcissistic behaviors is the concept of narcissistic supply. Narcissists have an insatiable need for attention, admiration, and validation from others. They seek out individuals who provide this narcissistic supply, and when they no longer receive it, they can become manipulative and abusive. Gaslighting is one way narcissists maintain control over their victims and ensure a steady supply of validation.

Covert narcissism is another aspect of narcissistic behavior that is important to understand. Unlike overt narcissists who display grandiose and attention-seeking behaviors, covert narcissists are more subtle in their manipulation tactics. They often present themselves as victims and use covert ways to control, manipulate, and gaslight their victims. Understanding covert narcissism helps victims recognize the signs of manipulation and protect themselves from further harm.

By exploring these psychological theories behind narcissistic behaviors and their tie to gaslighting, victims can gain clarity and understanding of their experiences. It helps victims realize that they are not to blame for the abuse they have endured and empowers them to reclaim their power. Education is a powerful tool enabling individuals to protect themselves from further harm and regain their self-worth and confidence.

In the next part of this chapter, we will delve deeper into the definitions and workings of narcissistic personality disorder and covert narcissism. By understanding the characteristics and traits associated with these disorders, victims can recognize the patterns of manipulation and abuse more quickly. This knowledge is vital to breaking free from the cycle of gaslighting and reclaiming their sense of self. So, let's explore the intricacies of these disorders and shed light on the covert tactics of the manipulator.

Understanding narcissistic personality disorder (NPD) and covert narcissism is essential when deciphering the mind of a manipulator. These disorders are characterized by a pervasive pattern of grandiosity, a need for admiration, and a lack of empathy. While individuals with NPD exhibit overt arrogant and attention-seeking behaviors, those with covert narcissism are more subtle in their manipulation tactics. They may appear self-sacrificing and empathetic on the surface, but underneath lies a deep-seated need for control and validation.

Narcissistic personality disorder can manifest in various ways. Still, some common traits include an exaggerated sense of self-importance, a preoccupation with fantasies of unlimited success, power, brilliance, beauty, or ideal love, and an expectation of special treatment. Covert narcissism, on the other hand, is characterized by a fragile self-esteem masked by a facade of humility and selflessness. These individuals often manipulate others through guilt, pity, and a false sense of martyrdom.

Gaslighting, a psychological manipulation tactic employed by narcissists, plays a significant role in maintaining control over their victims. Gaslighting involves distorting the victim's perception of reality, making them doubt their sanity and judgment. By doing so, the narcissist can assert their dominance and maintain power over their victim.

To protect oneself from further psychological abuse, it is crucial to understand the workings of NPD and covert narcissism. Individuals can reclaim power and establish healthy boundaries by recognizing the common traits and manipulation tactics associated with these disorders. Education is essential in empowering victims and enabling them to identify and navigate toxic relationships.

Learning about NPD and covert narcissism not only aids in recognizing manipulative behaviors but also provides insight into the underlying psychological mechanisms that drive them. By understanding the motivations behind a narcissist's actions, individuals can gain clarity and perspective, realizing that the abuse is not a result of their flaws or shortcomings but rather a reflection of the narcissist's insecurities and deep-seated wounds.

Recognizing the signs of NPD and covert narcissism allows individuals to take a proactive approach to protect themselves from further harm. With knowledge, victims can develop effective coping mechanisms, establish boundaries, and seek support from therapists, support groups, and other resources. By actively engaging in their healing journey, individuals can break free from the cycle of abuse and reclaim their sense of self-worth and agency.

Gain Insight and Reclaim Your Power

To defend yourself from further psychological abuse, it is crucial to arm yourself with knowledge and insight. Education is a powerful tool that empowers victims to protect themselves and reclaim their power. By learning about the psychological theories behind narcissistic behaviors, you can gain valuable insight into the manipulator's mind and the dynamics of abuse and manipulation.

Understanding the intricacies of narcissistic personality disorder (NPD) and covert narcissism is a crucial step toward breaking free from the toxic cycle. By familiarizing yourself with these terms and their definitions, you can begin to make sense of your experiences and recognize the manipulation tactics used against you.

Narcissistic personality disorder is a mental health condition characterized by a grandiose sense of self-importance, a constant need for admiration, and a lack of empathy for others. Individuals with NPD often manipulate and exploit others for their gain, emotionally and psychologically abusing those around them. By recognizing the signs and symptoms of NPD, you can identify when you are dealing with a narcissist and take steps to protect yourself.

Covert narcissism, on the other hand, refers to a more subtle and insidious form of narcissism. Covert narcissists may appear outwardly humble and self-effacing but are deeply entrenched in a pattern of manipulation and control. By understanding the workings of covert narcissism, you can better detect and navigate the covert manipulation techniques used against you.

One of the most insidious tactics employed by narcissists is gaslighting. Gaslighting is a psychological manipulation technique used to distort the victim's reality and make them doubt their perceptions and experiences. By learning about the psychological mechanisms behind gaslighting, you can begin to untangle the web of confusion and self-doubt that the narcissist has woven around you.

Ultimately, education empowers you to protect yourself from further harm. By gaining insight into the mind of the manipulator, you can reclaim your power and take control of your own life. The knowledge and understanding you acquire will provide the tools and strategies to set boundaries, recognize manipulation, and assertively confront abusive behavior.

It is important to remember that you are not alone in this journey. Many others have faced similar experiences and have come out stronger on the other side. You can build a network of understanding and resilience by educating yourself and seeking support from trusted individuals or groups.

In the following sections, we will delve deeper into the psychological theories behind narcissistic behaviors, explore the definitions of narcissistic personality disorder and covert narcissism, and provide you with practical strategies to defend yourself from further psychological abuse. You can reclaim your power and break free from manipulation through education and understanding.

Take Charge of Your Understanding and Power

Embracing the psychological theories that illuminate narcissistic behaviors and the intricacies of gaslighting is not merely an academic exercise; it is your shield against manipulation and your key to reclaiming autonomy. **Knowledge is your armor, and education is your sword**. By delving into the definitions and workings of narcissistic personality disorder and covert narcissism, you equip yourself with the tools to decode the cryptic language of manipulators and see through their façade.

Arm Yourself with Awareness and Vigilance

Remaining vigilant after learning about the mechanisms and characteristics of narcissistic abuse is your superpower. Recognizing the red flags and subtle cues that signify a toxic relationship empowers you to set boundaries and protect your emotional well-being. **Trust your instincts, and never underestimate the value of self-awareness**. Understanding the playbook of manipulators immunizes you against their twisted narratives and fosters confidence in your reality.

Forge Ahead with Resilience and Resolve

Armed with knowledge and awareness, you are better equipped to navigate the shadows of doubt. Lean into the strength of understanding and take decisive steps to reclaim your sense of self. **You are not alone**; countless others have walked this path and emerged stronger. Remember, the power to break free from the grasp of manipulation lies within you. **Embrace your journey to reclaim your fire and enter a future filled with self-assurance and authenticity.**

Chapter 8: Resilience in the Face of Gaslighting: Personal Victories

"Truth is not something outside to be discovered,

it is something inside to be realized."

Osho

From Shadows to Sunshine: Embracing the Journey of Healing

Gaslighting is a complex form of emotional abuse that leaves individuals questioning their reality, feeling isolated, and struggling with self-doubt. However, countless survivors have emerged stronger, wiser, and more empowered amidst these turbulent waters. Their stories are not just narratives; they're beacons of hope for anyone navigating the path of healing from narcissistic manipulation. The essence of these personal triumphs is central to understanding that no one is alone in their struggles and that recovery is not just possible—it's within reach.

Success stories are powerful because they prove that overcoming gaslighting is achievable. These narratives validate the feelings and experiences of those still in the throes of manipulation, proving that their struggles are real and surmountable. Through the lens of others' successes, individuals gain a clearer perspective on their situations, understanding that their reactions to gaslighting are justified and that there's light at the end of the tunnel.

Drawing inspiration from the journeys of others is invaluable. It is not merely about knowing that someone else has succeeded; it's about seeing a reflection of one's potential future. These stories paint a picture of what life can look like post-recovery: more self-assured, grounded in reality, and equipped with the tools to fend off manipulation. They serve as a roadmap for navigating one's journey, offering practical strategies distilled from the hardships and triumphs of those who walked the path before.

The significance of community and shared experiences in healing cannot be overstated. There's strength in numbers and solace in shared stories. Knowing others have faced similar challenges and emerged victorious helps dismantle the feeling of isolation that gaslighting often creates. It builds a network of support that fosters healing, encouraging individuals to share their stories, listen actively, and validate each other's experiences. This sense of belonging is instrumental in rebuilding the self-esteem that narcissistic manipulation seeks to destroy.

To truly benefit from these success stories, engaging actively with them is important. Reflect on the strategies that helped others, but also remember that healing is personal. The efficacy of different approaches can vary from one individual to another. Therefore, *staying open-minded and flexible is crucial*, as well as adapting insights from others' journeys to fit personal circumstances and needs.

Moreover, overcoming gaslighting is not just about moving past the abuse; it's about reclaiming one's fire—the inner strength, confidence, and self-belief that gaslighting seeks to extinguish. Success stories are a testament to the fact that this inner fire can be protected and grow stronger through the trials faced. They provide a glimmer of hope and a reflection of the resilience and strength present in every survivor.

In embracing these narratives, readers are reminded that their journey is not solitary. They're part of a larger movement—a collective rising from the ashes of manipulation, stronger and more united. Through shared stories of triumph, individuals find the inspiration to persevere and the practical wisdom to navigate their recovery. This chapter serves as a reminder: no one walks alone in the battle against gaslighting.

Success stories can be a powerful source of hope and validation for those who have experienced gaslighting. When individuals share their triumphs over gaslighting, it validates the experiences of others who have faced similar challenges and provides inspiration and motivation for healing and recovery.

Hearing about personal success stories can help individuals realize they are not alone in their struggles. It can be easy to feel isolated and misunderstood when gaslighting occurs, as the manipulator aims to undermine the victim's perception of reality and make them question their own experiences. But **by listening to others who have overcome gaslighting, individuals can gain a sense of community and validation, knowing that their experiences are valid and shared by others.**

Success stories also offer hope. They show that it is possible to heal and recover from the damaging effects of gaslighting. It can be difficult to imagine a life free from the manipulation and doubt that gaslighting creates, but success stories provide tangible evidence that healing is possible. These stories act as a symbol of resilience, reminding individuals that they possess the strength and inner resources to overcome their challenges.

Moreover, success stories can inspire individuals on their healing journey. They demonstrate the power of resilience and recovery, showing that rebuilding a sense of self-worth, trusting one's judgment, and creating healthy relationships is possible. By sharing their stories of growth and transformation, individuals who have overcome gaslighting can inspire others to embark on their healing journey.

Success stories also offer practical insights and strategies for overcoming gaslighting. Hearing about the techniques and approaches others have used to reclaim their power and assert their boundaries can provide individuals with practical tools they can implement. These stories can offer guidance and encouragement, giving individuals the confidence they need to heal.

Deriving inspiration from the journeys of resilience and recovery is like finding a guiding light in the darkness. These personal stories can ignite a spark of hope, reminding us that we are not alone in our struggles against gaslighting. We are reminded of our strength and resilience when we hear about others who have faced similar challenges and triumphed over them. These stories validate our experiences, reassuring us that what we have been through is genuine and not imagined.

As we read about others who have overcome gaslighting, we believe in the possibility of healing and transformation. These stories serve as a source of hope, demonstrating that reclaiming our sense of self and rebuilding our lives is indeed possible. They demonstrate light at the end of the tunnel, even when it may seem impossibly far away.

These journeys of resilience and recovery serve as a source of inspiration, motivating us to continue our healing journey. They show us that it is possible to rise above the manipulation and regain control of our lives. By learning from those who have successfully navigated through gaslighting, we gain valuable insights and strategies to apply to our situations.

Perhaps most importantly, these stories emphasize the significance of community and shared experiences in healing.

They remind us that we are not alone in our struggles and that others understand what we have been through. This sense of connection and solidarity can provide immense comfort and strength as we continue our healing journey.

Through these personal success stories, we are reminded that we have the power to overcome gaslighting. We are not victims but survivors who can rise above the manipulation and reclaim our lives. These stories inspire us to tap into our innate resilience and courage, empowering us to regain power.

In the next section, we will explore the importance of community and shared experiences in healing. We will explore how finding support and connecting with others can accelerate our healing process. By learning from one another and offering support, we can create a network of resilience that strengthens us individually and as a collective. So, let us continue on this resilience journey, armed with the knowledge that we are not alone and that healing is possible.

Understand the Significance of Community and Shared Experiences in Healing

Recovering from gaslighting can be a challenging and isolating journey, but it doesn't have to be a lonely one. One of the most powerful tools in healing from gaslighting is the sense of community and shared experiences. When we connect with others who have faced similar challenges, we gain validation, support, and a renewed sense of hope. The stories of resilience and recovery from those who have triumphed over gaslighting can inspire us to keep going, even in our darkest moments.

Community plays a vital role in healing from gaslighting because it allows us to find a safe space where we can openly share our experiences without fear of judgment or invalidation. By connecting with others who have gone through similar experiences, we realize that we are not alone in our struggles. This solidarity can be incredibly empowering and help us regain our self-esteem and confidence.

When we hear the stories of individuals who have successfully navigated through gaslighting, we gain validation for our own experiences. It can be challenging to trust our perceptions and judgment after being manipulated and gaslit for an extended period. However, hearing others share similar experiences can remind us that our feelings and reactions are valid and that we are not to blame for the abuse we endured.

These success stories also provide us with a roadmap for healing. We can learn from the strategies and techniques others have used to overcome gaslighting and incorporate them into our journey toward recovery. Hearing about their steps to regain their sense of self and establish healthy boundaries can empower us to take action in our own lives.

Furthermore, community support can offer us a sense of belonging and acceptance essential for healing. Often, survivors of gaslighting may feel isolated and misunderstood by friends or family who haven't experienced such manipulation. Connecting with others who have been through similar experiences can provide a level of understanding and empathy that is hard to find elsewhere. These connections show us the strength and encouragement to continue our healing journey.

In a society that often downplays or dismisses emotional abuse, community support becomes even more crucial. By coming together and sharing our stories, we can raise awareness about gaslighting and help others who may still be trapped in abusive situations. We can break the cycle of silence and provide a sign of hope for those searching for a way out.

A Sign of Hope and Validation

Amidst gaslighting, personal success stories shine as guiding lights of hope and validation for those navigating manipulation's shadows. These stories illuminate the path to healing, showing that overcoming gaslighting is not a far-fetched dream but an achievable reality. Each tale of triumph reinforces that **recovery is possible** and that one can reclaim one's sense of self and agency.

Nurturing Resilience and Recovery

Witnessing the **journeys of resilience** from individuals who have braved the storm of gaslighting can ignite a spark within those still struggling. These stories showcase the **strength and perseverance** it takes to emerge from manipulation. They remind us that setbacks are not defeats but opportunities to grow and evolve, pushing us closer to a place of healing and self-empowerment.

The Power of Shared Experiences

A sense of community is formed through the shared experiences of overcoming gaslighting. Knowing that others have walked a similar path and emerged stronger can provide comfort and encouragement. This collective understanding fosters a supportive environment where individuals can **share, learn, and heal** together. In this community of survivors, the shadows of doubt dissipate, allowing the light of validation, hope, and resilience to shine.

Chapter 9: The Language of Liberation: A Gaslighting Glossary

"The human mind, once stretched by a new idea,

never returns to its original dimensions."

Oliver Wendell Holmes Jr.

Unlocking the Cipher: Understanding Gaslighting's Complex Web

Gaslighting and narcissistic manipulation often weave a complex web of confusion, leaving victims questioning their sanity, reality, and self-worth. The very essence of gaslighting is to disorient and control, making it vital for those affected to recognize the signs and arm themselves with knowledge. This requires understanding the specific language and concepts that define such toxic dynamics. By demystifying key terms and ideas, individuals gain the power to see through manipulation, identify abusive behavior, and initiate steps toward recovery and empowerment.

A well-defined glossary of terms related to gaslighting and narcissistic abuse serves as an essential guide in navigating through the shadows of doubt. It's not just about learning new words; it's about enhancing one's understanding of the mechanics behind emotional manipulation. Recognizing terms like 'hoovering,' 'flying monkeys', or 'love bombing' transforms them from mere jargon into clear indicators of manipulative behaviors. This knowledge empowers victims to articulate their experiences, making it easier to seek help and support.

With the proper terminology, individuals are better prepared to counteract gaslighting's effects. It's one thing to feel that something in a relationship is off; it's another to be able to name the specific tactics being used. This not only aids in personal healing but also in educating others, fostering a broader awareness of narcissistic abuse. **Understanding the language of gaslighting equips individuals with the tools needed to effectively discuss and heal from their experiences.**

Moreover, reclaiming one's narrative is a critical step in overcoming the effects of gaslighting. Victims can rebuild their self-esteem and assert their reality by defining and owning the terms that describe their experiences. Language is powerful—it shapes thought and perception. When someone can accurately label what they've been through, they reclaim a sense of control over their story.

Practical strategies for identifying and responding to gaslighting are also essential. Simple, actionable advice can make a significant difference for those trapped in the cycle of manipulation. For instance, keeping a journal of events or conversations can help maintain a clear record of reality, countering the gaslighter's attempts to distort it. Setting clear boundaries and consistently enforcing them signals to the abuser that their tactics are recognized and will not be tolerated.

Encouragement to take control of one's situation is key. Victims of gaslighting often feel powerless, but understanding the dynamics at play can spark a sense of agency. With a clear grasp of gaslighting's language, individuals can start to untangle the manipulation, setting the stage for reclaiming their independence and self-worth.

Emphasis on the innate ability for emotional mastery and overcoming challenges is fundamental. Everyone possesses the strength to recover from manipulation and abuse. However, unlocking this strength requires clarity, knowledge, and support. By exploring gaslighting's glossary, individuals embark on a journey towards self-empowerment, equipped with the language that lights the path out of darkness.

Gaslighting is a subtle and insidious form of emotional manipulation that can leave its victims feeling confused, doubting their reality, and questioning their sanity. To understand gaslighting and its effects, it is important to demystify key terms and concepts related to this form of abuse.

One important term to understand is "*gaslighting*" itself. Coined from a play and subsequent film titled Gas Light, gaslighting manipulates someone into questioning their reality. Gaslighters often twist the truth, deny their actions or words, and make their victims feel as though they are the ones who are crazy or at fault. Understanding that gaslighting is a deliberate tactic used by manipulative individuals can help victims recognize when it is happening to them.

Another concept related to gaslighting is "*narcissistic abuse.*" Narcissistic abuse occurs when someone with narcissistic personality traits uses emotional manipulation to control and diminish their partner or loved one. They may use tactics such as gaslighting, devaluation, and projection to undermine their victim's sense of self-worth and keep them under their control.

A key aspect of gaslighting and narcissistic abuse is the "cycle of abuse." This cycle typically consists of three phases: the idealization or "love bombing" phase, where the abuser showers their victim with love and affection; the devaluation or "gaslighting" phase, where the abuser begins to erode their victim's sense of self and manipulate their reality; and the discard phase, where the abuser either ends the relationship or pushes their victim away emotionally. Understanding this cycle can help victims recognize when they are being manipulated and take steps to protect themselves.

Gaslighting often involves manipulation of the victim's perception of reality. "Cognitive dissonance" is a term used to describe the mental discomfort a person experiences when their beliefs or perceptions conflict with each other. Gaslighters often exploit this cognitive dissonance by making their victims question their memories, perceptions, and even their sanity.

Another term to be familiar with is "*triangulation.*" Triangulation occurs when an abusive person brings a third party into the relationship, often to create jealousy or competition. This tactic can further erode the victim's self-esteem and make them feel insecure and unworthy.

Understanding these key terms and concepts related to gaslighting and emotional manipulation is essential for anyone who has experienced or is currently in a toxic relationship. It can help victims recognize the signs of abuse, set boundaries, and reclaim their sense of self-worth. By gaining knowledge and understanding, individuals can empower themselves to break free from the cycle of abuse and regain control over their lives.

Recognizing, Understanding, and Countering Manipulative Tactics

Gaslighting dynamics can be incredibly subtle and difficult to detect. This section will enhance your understanding of these dynamics, equipping you to recognize better and counteract them. By shedding light on the manipulative tactics often employed by gaslighters, we can empower ourselves to regain control of our lives and protect our emotional well-being.

One common gaslighting tactic is denial. Gaslighters will often deny events or conversations that have taken place, causing the victim to question their memory and perception of reality. This can lead to a profound sense of self-doubt and confusion. By recognizing this manipulation tactic, we can trust our own experiences and stand firm in our truth.

Another key dynamic of gaslighting is the use of deflection. When confronted with their harmful behavior, gaslighters will often deflect blame onto their victims, making them feel guilty or responsible for the relationship's dysfunction. By understanding this tactic, we can refuse to accept blame for something that is not our fault and set healthy boundaries in our relationships.

Gaslighters also engage in manipulation through distortion of the truth. They may revise or exaggerate details of past events, causing us to question our perception of reality. By being aware of this tactic, we can trust our instincts and seek validation from trusted friends or professionals who can provide an objective perspective.

Another important aspect of gaslighting dynamics is the gradual erosion of self-confidence. Gaslighters will systematically chip away at our self-esteem, making us doubt our worth and capabilities. By recognizing this manipulation tactic, we can rebuild our self-confidence and surround ourselves with people who uplift and support us.

Gaslighters also exploit our vulnerabilities and insecurities. By targeting our weaknesses, they can exert control over us and keep us trapped in toxic relationships. By understanding this dynamic, we can identify our vulnerabilities and work on strengthening them, making us less susceptible to manipulation.

Lastly, gaslighting often involves using gaslighters to project their behaviors onto their victims. By accusing us of being irrational, emotionally unstable, or even manipulative, gaslighters can deflect attention away from their actions and maintain control over the narrative. By recognizing projection as a manipulation tactic, we can separate ourselves from these false accusations and reclaim our self-worth.

Understanding the dynamics of gaslighting is the first step towards countering its effects and regaining control over our lives. By recognizing these manipulation tactics, we can trust our perception of reality, set healthy boundaries, rebuild our self-esteem, and reclaim our sense of self. Armed with this knowledge, we can empower ourselves to break free from the cycle of gaslighting and cultivate fulfilling, respectful relationships.

Equip Yourself with the Language of Liberation

To effectively heal from gaslighting and emotional manipulation, it is crucial to have the language to understand and discuss your experiences. By equipping yourself with a gaslighting glossary, you can demystify the terms and concepts that often surround narcissistic abuse. This understanding will enhance your comprehension of the dynamics and empower you to identify signs, set boundaries, and reclaim your self-worth.

One key term to grasp is gaslighting itself. Gaslighting is a manipulative tactic used by narcissists and abusers to make you question your reality and doubt your perceptions. It is a form of psychological manipulation that undermines your confidence, leaving you feeling confused, invalidated, and uncertain of yourself. You can regain control over your thoughts and emotions by recognizing gaslighting for what it is.

Another important concept to understand is projection. Projection occurs when someone attributes their negative traits, behaviors, or feelings to another person. This defense mechanism allows the gaslighter to avoid taking responsibility for their actions and instead project their faults onto their victim. By recognizing projection, you can separate yourself from the false narratives imposed upon you.

Boundaries are another essential aspect of healing from gaslighting. Gaslighters often violate boundaries by invading your personal space, disregarding your autonomy, and belittling your needs and wants. By learning to set clear boundaries and assertively communicate them, you can reclaim your power and protect yourself from further manipulation.

Gaslighters frequently use invalidation to make you doubt your thoughts, feelings, and experiences. Invalidating statements such as "*You're overreacting*" or "*You're just being too sensitive*" dismiss your emotions and undermine reality. By recognizing invalidation, you can begin to validate your own experiences and feelings, rebuilding your self-esteem and self-trust.

Another crucial term is triangulation. Triangulation occurs when a gaslighter involves a third person, usually someone close to you, to manipulate and control you. They use this person to destabilize your perceptions further, creating a dynamic where you constantly feel like you must compete for attention, validation, or affection. By understanding triangulation, you can recognize and break free from this toxic cycle of manipulation.

Discarding is the final stage of a gaslighting relationship, where the abuser ultimately discards or devalues the victim. This can leave you feeling broken, worthless, and confused. By recognizing discarding for what it is, you can begin to understand that the devaluation and discard are not a reflection of your worthiness but rather a manipulation tactic used by the abuser.

By familiarizing yourself with these terms and concepts, you will be equipped to discuss and heal from your gaslighting experiences effectively. The gaslighting glossary provides you with a language of liberation, enabling you to articulate and understand the dynamics of narcissistic abuse. With this knowledge, you can reclaim your power, rebuild your self-esteem, and cultivate healthy, respectful relationships. Remember, you are not alone in your experiences, and a support community is ready to stand with you on your journey to healing.

Understanding Leads to Empowerment

As we come to the end of our exploration into the nuanced language surrounding gaslighting and emotional manipulation, it becomes clear that **demystifying key terms is the first step** toward breaking free from the chains of doubt and manipulation. By enhancing our understanding of these concepts, we equip ourselves with a powerful tool to recognize and counteract toxic dynamics effectively.

Mastering the Terminology

As we've dived into it, the language of liberation serves as a guiding light through the murky waters of manipulation. Knowing these terms and their implications, we can **better navigate through the shadows** that once clouded our judgment and sense of self-worth. Understanding concepts like gaslighting, love bombing, and projection is not just about definitions; it's about **reclaiming our power**.

Embracing Your Voice

With this newfound vocabulary, you are not merely a passive observer in your journey toward healing; you are an active participant, an advocate for your well-being. Through this chapter, we've provided you with the linguistic toolkit necessary to confidently engage in conversations about your experiences and seek support when needed. Remember, **knowledge is power**.

Walk Tall, Speak Loud

As you close this chapter, carry with you the understanding that **your voice matters**—it is valid, heard, and respected. Use the language of liberation to decode past hurts and pave the way for a future based on authenticity and self-empowerment. Stand tall, **speak your truth boldly**, and continue on your journey towards reclaiming your sense of self.

Chapter 10: The Strength of Unity: Building Supportive Communities

"He who has a why to live can bear almost any how."

Friedrich Nietzsche

Unlocking the Power of Communal Healing

Healing from the psychological scars left by narcissistic manipulation, especially gaslighting, is undeniably a challenging journey. The subtle yet profound impact of being continuously undermined can make one doubt one's reality, leading to a long road to rebuilding self-esteem and trust. However, the path to reclaiming your autonomy and inner fire doesn't have to be solitary. **Supportive communities, both online and in-**

person, present a powerful avenue for healing and empowerment.

One of the core benefits of engaging with supportive communities is the validation they provide. For many survivors of gaslighting, the most crippling aspect is the isolation – the feeling that you're alone in your experiences. However, within communities of individuals who have faced similar battles, your experiences are recognized and deeply understood. This validation can be incredibly healing, reminding you that your feelings and perceptions are valid.

Moreover, sharing your story and strategies for overcoming gaslighting in these safe spaces can be cathartic and educational. Articulating your experiences not only helps in processing trauma but also aids in the identification of manipulation tactics and recovery strategies. Learning from fellow survivors provides unique insights and practical advice that can be instrumental in your healing journey. These narratives often include setting boundaries, recognizing gaslighting early on, and rebuilding self-esteem.

Finding the right support group, therapist, or advocacy organization is crucial to this process. It's essential to seek out spaces that resonate with your specific needs and where you feel comfortable and secure. Online support groups offer accessibility and anonymity, which can be particularly helpful in the early stages of recovery. On the other hand, in-person communities provide a sense of tangible support and connection that can be incredibly affirming.

Guidance on how to navigate these resources is key. Start by identifying your primary needs: Do you seek emotional support, practical advice, or both? Once clear, research extensively. For online communities, look for forums and social media groups with active moderation and a clear focus on recovery from narcissistic abuse. When seeking therapy, prioritize professionals experienced in dealing with trauma and psychological manipulation.

Embarking on the road to recovery is a testament to your strength and resilience. Remember, you don't have to walk this path alone. Joining supportive communities can significantly enhance your healing process, providing tools and strategies for dealing with past trauma and fostering connections that inspire and empower. Through these shared spaces, survivors can find their voice, reaffirm their reality, and, most importantly, reignite their inner fire.

Supportive communities emphasize the collective strength in shared experiences and the healing power of being understood. They serve as a reminder that, while the journey may be challenging, regeneration and empowerment are within reach. Engaging actively with these groups can transform your healing journey, turning a path of individual struggle into communal triumph.

Supportive communities, both online and offline, can play a crucial role in the healing process for survivors of gaslighting. These communities offer a safe space for individuals to share their experiences, gain validation, and build connections with others who have gone through similar situations. Whether through online support groups or in-person meetups, joining these communities can provide healing benefits from gaslighting and reclaiming one's sense of self.

One of the key benefits of joining a supportive community is the validation it offers. Gaslighting can be an incredibly isolating experience, with victims often doubting their reality and feeling like they are going crazy. Connecting with others who have had similar experiences can help survivors realize that they are not alone and that their feelings and perceptions are valid. Hearing stories from others who have been through similar situations can provide a sense of validation and help individuals understand that they are not to blame for the gaslighting they have experienced.

Supportive communities also offer a valuable resource for healing and recovery. By sharing their experiences and listening to the stories and advice of others, survivors can gain insights and strategies for overcoming the effects of gaslighting. These communities can provide a wealth of information and resources, including books, articles, and websites that address the topic of gaslighting and offer guidance for healing. Through these resources, individuals can be educated about gaslighting and develop effective strategies for rebuilding their self-esteem and reclaiming their sense of self.

In addition to validation and resources, joining a supportive community can provide a much-needed sense of belonging and connection. Gaslighting can leave survivors feeling isolated and disconnected from others, as their experiences are often invalidated or dismissed. Individuals can find a sense of belonging and support by joining a community of understanding individuals, therapists, and fellow survivors. These communities can be a source of empowerment and strength as survivors share their stories, offer support, and encourage one another in their healing journeys.

Online support groups and advocacy organizations offer an accessible platform for survivors to connect with others and seek advice. These virtual communities provide a safe space for individuals to share their experiences anonymously and receive support from a diverse group. Online forums and chat rooms allow survivors to ask questions, seek advice, and share their stories with others who have been through similar experiences. Similarly, advocacy organizations can provide resources, educational materials, and even opportunities for survivors to participate in advocacy efforts, raising awareness about gaslighting and supporting others in their healing journey.

Overall, joining supportive online and offline communities can be immensely beneficial for healing from gaslighting. These communities offer validation, resources, and a sense of belonging that can empower survivors and help them reclaim themselves. By connecting with others who have been through similar experiences and learning from their stories and advice, survivors can find the support and understanding they need to heal and move forward. In the next section, we will explore some of the experiences and strategies shared within these safe spaces, offering insights into overcoming gaslighting and reclaiming one's power.

Joining supportive communities, whether online or offline, can be incredibly beneficial for healing from gaslighting. These communities provide a safe space for survivors to share their experiences, gain validation, and receive support from others who have faced similar challenges. By connecting with understanding individuals, therapists, and fellow survivors, individuals can feel a sense of belonging and empowerment as they navigate their healing journey.

Sharing experiences and strategies within these safe spaces can be compelling. Being able to openly discuss the effects of gaslighting and the steps taken to overcome it can help survivors feel heard and understood. It also allows for exchanging valuable insights and advice, as different individuals may have discovered unique strategies that have worked for them. By sharing these experiences, survivors can gain new perspectives and potentially find solutions they may not have considered.

In safe spaces, individuals can learn and implement strategies for overcoming gaslighting. These strategies may include setting boundaries, recognizing manipulation tactics, and building self-esteem. Hearing about the experiences of others can help survivors validate their own emotions and experiences, as gaslighting often leaves individuals questioning their reality and feelings. It can also inspire and motivate individuals to take action and reclaim their power.

One of the key benefits of joining supportive communities is the sense of community and connection it provides. Gaslighting can be an isolating experience, as it often involves the manipulation and isolation of the victim. By connecting with others who have gone through similar experiences, survivors can find a support network that understands their unique challenges. This sense of community can provide comfort, encouragement, and motivation throughout the healing process.

Supportive communities can be found both online and offline. Online support groups and advocacy organizations provide platforms for survivors to connect and seek advice. These groups often have dedicated forums or social media groups where survivors can share their experiences and engage in discussions. Offline support can be found through therapy or support groups that meet in person, where survivors can have face-to-face interactions and support.

Finding the right supportive community is essential for effective healing. It's important to seek out communities that align with individual needs, values, and experiences. Finding a supportive community that feels safe and understanding is crucial, whether it's an online forum, a therapy group, or a local support group. Researching and exploring different options can help individuals find the right fit for their needs.

Support groups, therapists, and advocacy organizations can play a vital role in the healing process for those who have experienced gaslighting. These supportive communities offer a safe space for survivors to share their experiences, seek guidance and validation, and connect with others who have experienced similar situations. In this third part of the chapter, we will guide you in finding the right support groups, therapists, and advocacy organizations to aid in your healing journey.

Finding the right support group is important in building a network of understanding individuals who can provide validation and support. Online support groups can be an excellent option for those who may not have access to in-person groups or prefer the anonymity they provide. Look for groups specifically focused on gaslighting or narcissistic abuse, as they will have members who can truly empathize with your experiences. It can also be helpful to join groups with a mix of survivors at different stages of healing, as this allows for a diverse range of perspectives and insights.

In addition to online support groups, therapy can also be an invaluable resource for healing from gaslighting. A therapist who specializes in narcissistic abuse or trauma can provide a safe environment for you to process your experiences, validate your feelings, and develop coping strategies. When seeking a therapist, consider reaching out to local domestic violence centers, as they often have resources and referrals for therapists who are experienced in working with survivors of gaslighting and emotional abuse.

Advocacy organizations focused on gaslighting and narcissistic abuse can offer a wealth of resources and support. These organizations often provide online forums, educational materials, and articles with strategies and insights for healing. They may also offer workshops or webinars that cover topics such as setting boundaries, rebuilding self-esteem, and developing healthy relationships. Connecting with an advocacy organization can help you feel empowered and supported as you navigate the healing process.

When seeking out these supportive communities, it's essential to trust your instincts and ensure that the groups, therapists, and organizations align with your needs and values. Take the time to research and read reviews or testimonials from others who have engaged with these resources. Consider reaching out to members of the support groups or organizations to ask questions and get a sense of the community. Finding the proper support is a personal journey, and what works for one person may not work for another. Trust yourself to make the right choices.

You can access valuable resources, connections, and validation for your healing journey by joining supportive online and in-person communities. Support groups, therapists, and advocacy organizations can provide a sense of belonging and empowerment as you navigate the challenges of recovering from gaslighting. Remember, you are not alone; reaching out to these communities can offer the support and understanding you deserve.

Building and connecting within supportive communities, whether online or offline, can be a source of immense strength and validation as you navigate the aftermath of gaslighting. **Joining these communities offers a sense of belonging and provides invaluable resources and connections to support your healing journey.** Through shared experiences and strategies, you can gain insights into overcoming gaslighting in safe spaces. **These spaces offer a sanctuary where you can assert your reality and feel validated in your emotions and experiences.**

In the digital realm, online support groups and social platforms can serve as lifelines, offering a bridge to others who have walked a similar path. You can find understanding ears, empathetic hearts, and practical advice to regain footing here. These online resources provide a 24/7 support system, ensuring you are never isolated in your battle against gaslighting.

In your physical community, whether through therapy groups or local support networks, you can forge connections that transcend the digital divide. The warmth of human interaction, the comfort of shared physical space, and the power of face-to-face conversations can provide a different healing balm. These personal interactions remind you that you are not alone and that shared strength makes healing possible.

Remember, finding the right support group, therapist, or advocacy organization is not just about seeking help; it's about reclaiming your power and prioritizing your well-being. Surrounding yourself with individuals who understand, uplift, and empower you is crucial in your healing process. You can rebuild your self-esteem, trust your reality, and emerge stronger through these connections.

Chapter 11: Celebrating the Journey: Acknowledging Progress and Resilience

"When someone tries to manipulate you into doubting your sanity,it's a reflection of their desperation, not your weakness."

Unknown

Every Victory Counts: The Power of Celebrating Progress

The journey out of the shadow of gaslighting and into the light of personal autonomy and self-recognition is fraught with challenges and obstacles. Yet, accumulating small victories along this path paves the way for profound healing and transformation. Recognizing and celebrating these victories is not just an act of self-love; it is a crucial strategy for rebuilding the confidence and self-esteem that gaslighting seeks to erode. This chapter delves into the transformative power of acknowledging every step forward, no matter how minor it might seem, and how this practice can fortify resilience and accelerate recovery.

Small victories are the milestones of your journey. In the aftermath of manipulation, recognizing your progress can often feel daunting. Yet, these moments, from setting a boundary to simply saying "*no*," mark significant strides in reclaiming your sense of self. By celebrating these acts, you acknowledge your progress and reinforce your belief in your ability to overcome and heal. It's a testament to your strength and an affirmation that you are moving in the right direction, guided by your light.

Cultivating a culture of appreciation for oneself is a cornerstone of healing from narcissistic manipulation. It shifts the focus from what's been lost to what's being reclaimed and grown. This shift is pivotal. It encourages a nurturing attitude toward oneself, fostering an environment where self-compassion flourishes. Just as importantly, it dismantles the narrative imposed by the gaslighter, piece by piece, replacing it with your own story of resilience and recovery.

Building confidence and self-esteem comes with recognizing your worth and the significance of your journey. *Every act of resistance against manipulation, every moment of self-care, and every boundary set is a declaration of your worth.* These are the bricks and mortar of the new, resilient structure you build around your sense of self. Each acknowledgment of progress, no matter how small, adds to this structure, making it stronger and more resilient against future challenges.

Moreover, celebrating progress fosters a supportive inner dialogue, replacing critical or demeaning internal messages with encouragement and support. This new dialogue is crucial for those recovering from gaslighting, as it helps counteract the negative self-beliefs instilled by the abuser. It's about rewriting the narrative within your mind—a narrative that champions your strength, progress, and unyielding resolve to heal and thrive.

Adopting practical strategies to recognize and celebrate progress can range from journaling your achievements, no matter how small, to sharing your victories with a supportive friend or therapist. It can also involve setting aside time for self-care as a reward for milestones reached. The key is to create a tangible record of your journey— a map of victories that leads you back to yourself.

Cultivating gratitude towards oneself enriches the healing journey and ensures that each step taken is cherished. This approach does not require monumental achievements; instead, it thrives on accumulating small, daily acts of bravery and self-love. It's about seeing the value in the struggle and the growth that emerges from it.

By celebrating each victory, regardless of size, individuals on the path to recovery from gaslighting can build resilient self-esteem and a confident outlook that propels them forward. It's a journey that is as much about reclaiming your fire as it is about recognizing the sparks that have been there all along, guiding you out of the darkness. By acknowledging and celebrating each step, you illuminate your path and affirm your strength, worth, and unbreakable spirit on this journey of healing and empowerment.

Recognize the Importance of Celebrating Small Victories in the Recovery Process

Recovering from gaslighting is a complex and challenging journey, filled with ups and downs. It is easy to feel overwhelmed and discouraged by the long road ahead. That is why it is essential to recognize and celebrate the small victories along the way. Each achievement, no matter how small, is a step forward in reclaiming your sense of self and breaking free from the effects of gaslighting.

Acknowledging and celebrating these small victories is crucial for several reasons. First, it builds confidence and self-esteem. Gaslighting can erode your self-confidence, leaving you questioning your worth and abilities. By celebrating even the tiniest accomplishments, you are reinforcing positive beliefs about yourself and your abilities. It serves as a reminder that you are capable and resilient.

Second, celebrating small victories provides a sense of accomplishment. Gaslighting often leaves you feeling defeated and helpless. However, each boundary you set, every act of self-care, and each step towards healing is a success worth celebrating. Recognizing these achievements lets you see your progress and how far you have come. It reminds you that you are stronger than you think and that you have the power to overcome the challenges you face.

Finally, celebrating small victories reinforces resilience and determination. Gaslighting takes a toll on your mental and emotional well-being, and it can be easy to give in to self-doubt and despair. However, by acknowledging and appreciating your progress, you are reinforcing your determination to break free from the grips of gaslighting. It gives you the strength and motivation to continue moving forward, even when the road gets tough.

So, take the time to celebrate each small victory on your path to recovery. Whether setting a boundary with a gaslighter, practicing self-care, or seeking support from loved ones, every step counts. Embrace these moments of triumph as opportunities for growth and healing. They are reminders that you are on the right path and have the power to reclaim your fire and live a life free from gaslighting.

How Can You Acknowledge and Appreciate Your Progress Today?

Building confidence and self-esteem is a key component of the recovery process from gaslighting. Acknowledging progress, no matter how small, is essential to reclaiming one's sense of self and regaining personal power. Often, when we have experienced gaslighting, we may feel like we have lost our footing and have little faith in our abilities and decisions. Celebrating small victories allows us to break free from this cycle of self-doubt and reaffirm our worth and resilience.

It is important to recognize that progress is not always linear. Healing takes time, and there will be moments of setbacks and challenges along the way. However, acknowledging even the most minor steps forward can cultivate a sense of accomplishment and motivation to keep moving forward. Each small victory, whether standing up for ourselves, setting boundaries, or practicing self-care, is a testament to our strength and determination.

One practical strategy for acknowledging progress is keeping a journal. This can be a space to reflect on and celebrate milestones, no matter how insignificant they may seem. It can be as simple as writing down a positive interaction or a moment when we trusted our instincts. By capturing these moments, we can see how far we have come, even when it may not feel like it in the present moment.

Another way to build confidence and self-esteem is through positive self-talk. Gaslighting often erodes our sense of self-worth, causing us to doubt our abilities and question our value. We can develop a more compassionate and empowering inner dialogue by consciously replacing negative self-talk with positive affirmations. This can be as simple as reminding ourselves of our strengths and achievements or practicing self-compassion during moments of self-doubt.

Additionally, surrounding ourselves with a support system of trusted friends, family, or professionals can significantly contribute to our sense of progress and self-esteem. These individuals can provide validation, encouragement, and perspective when needed. They can help us recognize and celebrate our accomplishments, reminding us that we are not alone.

We can rebuild our confidence and self-esteem by acknowledging progress and celebrating small victories. Each step forward, no matter how small, contributes to our personal growth and healing. Let us take the time to reflect on our achievements and appreciate our resilience. Through self-compassion and a supportive community, we can solidify our sense of self-worth and continue to reclaim our fire.

Cultivate a Culture of Appreciation and Self-Compassion on the Path to Healing

As you continue on your journey of recovery from gaslighting, it's essential to cultivate a culture of appreciation and self-compassion. These practices will reinforce your progress and improve your overall well-being and growth. You build confidence and self-esteem when you acknowledge and appreciate the steps you've taken, no matter how small they may seem. And when you show yourself compassion and understanding, you reinforce your resilience and determination to break free from the effects of gaslighting.

One way to cultivate an appreciation culture is to celebrate small victories. Take a moment to reflect on your progress so far, whether recognizing a gaslighting tactic, setting boundaries with a manipulative person, or practicing self-care. Each of these achievements is a step forward on your journey of healing. Celebrating these victories reinforces positive behaviors and builds momentum for further growth.

Furthermore, acknowledging your progress and achievements can boost your confidence and self-esteem. You see yourself in a new light when you recognize and appreciate your strengths and abilities. You realize that you have the power to overcome challenges and navigate through difficult situations. This newfound confidence will empower you to assert your boundaries, advocate for yourself, and create a life that aligns with your values and desires.

In addition to celebrating your victories, you must surround yourself with a supportive network of people who appreciate and value your progress. Seek out individuals who understand your experiences and can offer validation and encouragement. Share your achievements with them, whether it's a breakthrough in therapy or successfully implementing a new self-care practice. Their support and validation will reinforce your sense of accomplishment and remind you that you are not alone.

Practicing self-compassion is another essential aspect of cultivating a culture of appreciation. Gaslighting can leave you feeling unworthy, ashamed, and self-critical. But by showing yourself compassion and understanding, you counteract these negative beliefs and nurture a positive and loving relationship with yourself. Remember that healing is a process, and it's okay to have setbacks along the way. Treat yourself with kindness and gentleness, just as a dear friend would. Remind yourself that you are doing your best and that every step forward, no matter how small, is a testament to your resilience and strength.

To cultivate a culture of self-compassion, practice self-care regularly. Engage in activities that bring you joy and nurture your well-being. This could be anything from taking a bubble bath to enjoying a cup of tea while reading a book. Prioritize your needs and make time for self-care, even for just a few minutes each day. When you prioritize your well-being, you send a powerful message to yourself that you are worthy of love, care, and attention.

Embracing Growth and Resilience

Celebrating small victories is not merely a token gesture but an essential component of your healing journey. Every step you take toward recovery, no matter how small it may seem, deserves acknowledgment and praise. Recognizing and celebrating these moments fortifies your self-worth and strengthens your resolve to reclaim your power. Each boundary sets each act of self-care practiced, which contributes to the foundation of your resilience and growth.

Acknowledge Your Progress

Amidst the tumultuous aftermath of gaslighting, it's easy to overlook the progress you've made. Pause for a moment and reflect on how far you've come. Take note of all the strides you've taken in rebuilding yourself. Your progress, no matter how incremental, is a testament to your courage and determination. Acknowledge it, celebrate it, and let it fuel your journey forward.

Nurturing Self-Compassion

Cultivating a culture of appreciation and self-compassion is key to navigating the shadows of doubt. Embrace the kindness and understanding you readily offer others, and direct it inward. Practice self-compassion as a daily ritual, showering yourself with the same grace you extend to those you care for. In moments of self-doubt, remind yourself of your resilience and progress, reaffirming your worth and strength.

A Path Illuminated

As you traverse the path to healing, remember that each small victory is a beacon of light guiding you forward. Embrace these moments of celebration as affirmations of your growth and resilience. By acknowledging your progress, building your self-esteem, and nurturing self-compassion, you pave the way for a brighter, empowered future. Stand tall in the glow of your achievements, for they are the stepping stones to reclaiming your light and breaking free from the shadows of gaslighting.

Chapter 12: Words of Empowerment: Quotes and Affirmations

"We accept the love we think we deserve."

Stephen Chbosky

Transform Doubt into Empowerment

Healing from the psychological effects of gaslighting requires more than just the passage of time; it necessitates a proactive approach toward nurturing self-belief and resilience. **The journey of recovery** from narcissistic manipulation is fraught with challenges, including overcoming deep-seated doubts and insecurities. In this context, the influence of words—through motivational quotes and affirmations—emerges as a guiding light of hope and strength.

In recovery, **motivational quotes and affirmations** catalyze fostering a mindset of empowerment. These powerful tools are not mere collections of words but are profound expressions of human experiences that resonate deeply with individuals seeking to rebuild their lives. They inspire, uplift, and, most importantly, reinforce the belief in one's capability to overcome adversity. By internalizing these messages, individuals embarking on this journey can begin to view their experiences through a lens of strength rather than victimhood.

Positive self-talk plays a critical role in combating feelings of doubt and insecurity that are often magnified by experiences of gaslighting. The seeds of self-belief are sown through nurturing a dialogue of kindness and compassion with oneself. *Affirmations*, in particular, are instrumental in this process as reminders of one's worth, potential, and resilience. They encourage individuals to shift their focus from what they have endured to what lies within their power to change.

Integrating **encouraging words into daily routines** can have a transformative effect on one's mental and emotional well-being. This practice isn't about ignoring the realities of one's situation but about creating a space for hope and positivity to flourish. It's a way to start the day grounded in strength and end it with a reminder of one's progress. Embedding these empowering messages into daily life is a constant nudge toward healing and self-discovery.

The essence of healing lies in reclaiming one's fire—*the innate strength and spirit* that gaslighting attempts to dim. The journey is as much about rediscovery as it is about recovery. Words of empowerment play a vital role in this process, guiding individuals back to their core, where resilience, courage, and self-compassion reside. They act as a mirror, reflecting the unyielding strength within, often obscured by the shadows of doubt.

Empowerment through words is more than a strategy; it's a lifeline for those finding their way out of the darkness. By making these messages a staple in the healing journey, individuals can begin to dismantle the lies woven by gaslighting and step into a light of their own making. It's a step towards surviving and thriving with a renewed sense of self and an unwavering belief in one's worth and capabilities.

Action over passive contemplation is key—engaging with these strategies actively catalyzes real change. By fostering this empowerment mindset, individuals can navigate the often treacherous path of healing with a sense of direction and purpose. The journey from the shadows of doubt to reclaiming one's fire is arduous but armed with the power of words, and it's a journey that one does not have to walk alone.

Foster a Mindset of Empowerment Through Motivational Quotes and Affirmations

In healing from gaslighting, it can be incredibly beneficial to incorporate positive words of empowerment into our daily lives. Quotes and affirmations can uplift our spirits, motivate us to persevere, and remind us of our inherent strength and worthiness. By internalizing these positive messages, we can cultivate a mindset of empowerment that guides us through the challenges of healing.

Motivational quotes remind us that we are not alone in our struggles and that others have faced and overcome similar obstacles. They inspire us to take control of our lives, to trust our intuition, and to have faith in our ability to heal. On the other hand, affirmations are personal statements that we repeat to ourselves to counteract negative self-talk and build self-belief. By consciously choosing empowering affirmations, we can rewire our thinking patterns and cultivate a more positive and compassionate relationship with ourselves.

When selecting quotes and affirmations, choosing words that resonate with us is essential. What might be empowering for one person may not have the same effect on another. Trusting our intuition and selecting words that genuinely speak to our hearts and inspire us is important.

For example, a quote by Maya Angelou that resonates deeply with many survivors of gaslighting is, "*You may not control all the events that happen to you, but you can decide not to be reduced by them.*" This quote reminds us that although we may have experienced immense pain and trauma, we have the power to rise above it and not let it define us. It encourages us to take ownership of our healing journey and reclaim our sense of self.

Similarly, an empowering affirmation for overcoming gaslighting could be, "*I am worthy of love, respect, and understanding.*" By repeating this affirmation to ourselves regularly, we affirm our self-worth, remind ourselves of our inherent value, and reject the toxic messages we may have internalized from gaslighting.

Incorporating these quotes and affirmations into our daily routines is key to maximizing their impact. We can write them on sticky notes and place them where we see them frequently, such as on our bathroom mirror or computer screen. We can create a journal for recording quotes and affirmations and use it for reflection and motivation. We can even set reminders on our phones throughout the day, reminding us to repeat our chosen affirmations.

By fostering a mindset of empowerment through motivational quotes and affirmations, we can cultivate resilience, self-compassion, and self-belief. These powerful words remind us of our strength and resilience, guiding our journey of healing and self-discovery.

Positive self-talk is a powerful tool in combatting the feelings of doubt and insecurity that often accompany the healing process after experiencing gaslighting. By consciously choosing the language we speak to ourselves, we can reshape our inner dialogue and cultivate a more supportive and compassionate mindset. This practice allows us to challenge the negative beliefs and self-doubt that may have been instilled in us and empower ourselves with positive affirmations.

When we engage in positive self-talk, we actively counter the gaslighter's narrative that we are unworthy, inadequate, or crazy. We are rejecting their manipulation and reclaiming our power. Replacing those negative beliefs with positive affirmations reminds us of our inherent value, strength, and resilience. This shift in self-perception lays the foundation for healing and growth.

Affirmations are short, powerful statements repeated regularly to reinforce positive beliefs. They can be tailored to address specific areas of healing and growth. For example, if you are experiencing self-doubt, you might repeat affirmations such as *"I trust my instincts and make decisions with confidence"* or *"I am capable and deserving of love and respect."* By consistently repeating affirmations that align with your desired mindset, you are rewiring your brain to reinforce positive beliefs about yourself.

Incorporating positive self-talk into your daily routine can be as simple as starting each day with a few minutes of affirmations or as elaborate as creating a vision board filled with positive quotes and affirmations. The key is to make it a habit and to be consistent. By consistently engaging in positive self-talk, you reinforce the belief that you are worthy of love, respect, and happiness.

In addition to positive affirmations, it is also important to practice self-compassion. Healing from gaslighting can be a challenging and emotional journey, and it is essential to be kind to yourself along the way. Instead of berating yourself for mistakes or setbacks, remind yourself that healing takes time and that feeling a range of emotions is okay. Use self-compassionate language, such as *"I am doing the best I can"* or *"I deserve love and understanding."*

Remember, the power of positive self-talk lies in its ability to reshape our mindset and reinforce our inherent worth and value. Regularly engaging in positive self-talk and practicing self-compassion, we nurture our healing and reclaim our self-belief. So, let us put these tools into practice and empower ourselves with words of encouragement and support.

Incorporating encouraging words into our daily routines can uplift and inspire resilience as we navigate the healing process from gaslighting. By infusing our days with empowering quotes and affirmations, we can cultivate a mindset of self-belief and self-worth. These positive messages act as guiding lights, reminding us of our strength and capacity for growth. Let's explore how we can incorporate encouraging words into our daily routines to uplift and inspire resilience.

Start the day with intention: Begin each morning with a positive affirmation. Take a moment to repeat a phrase that promotes self-compassion, such as "I am worthy of love and respect." Allow the words to sink in and set the tone for the day ahead. By starting the day with intention, we can align ourselves with empowerment and cultivate a sense of inner strength.

Create reminders: Place post-it notes with inspirational quotes around your workspace, bathroom mirror, or refrigerator. These reminders can serve as gentle nudges throughout the day, reinforcing your worth and reminding you of your progress on your healing journey. Surrounding ourselves with positive messages helps counteract negative self-talk or lingering doubts.

Journaling: Incorporate encouraging words into your journaling practice. Write down quotes or affirmations that resonate with you and reflect on how they make you feel. Explore any resistance or challenges that come up as you internalize these messages. Allow your journal to become a safe space to express your thoughts and emotions, anchored by the supportive words you choose to include.

Affirmations on the go: Turn your commute, exercise routine, or household chores into opportunities for affirmation. Repeat positive statements to yourself silently or out loud. For example, you can affirm, "*I am resilient and capable of overcoming any challenge.*" By integrating affirmations into your daily activities, you infuse them with even more significant meaning and impact.

Seek inspiration: Surround yourself with inspirational sources such as books, podcasts, or online communities that share empowering quotes and stories of resilience. Engaging with these sources regularly can provide you with a steady stream of encouragement and motivation. Seek out narratives of individuals who have healed from gaslighting and transformed their lives, reminding yourself that you possess the strength to move forward.

Share the positivity: Spread the empowering words you encounter with those around you. Share your favorite quotes and affirmations with friends loved ones, or even on social media. By lifting others, you create a ripple effect of positivity and contribute to a supportive and encouraging community.

Incorporating encouraging words into our daily routines is a powerful tool for upliftment and resilience. By starting the day with intention, creating reminders, journaling, using affirmations on the go, seeking inspiration, and sharing positivity, we infuse our lives with the strength we need to heal and overcome challenges. Remember, you are not alone in your journey, and these empowering words remind you of your inherent worth and capacity for growth. Embrace the power of words and let them guide you towards a place of self-belief and empowerment. Keep moving forward, knowing you have the resilience to reclaim your sense of self.

Embracing Empowerment Through Words of Resilience

Quotes and affirmations have the remarkable power to shape our mindset, fueling us with the strength to overcome challenges and reaffirm our worth. In moments of doubt and vulnerability, these words act as glimmers of light, guiding us toward self-compassion, resilience, and empowerment.

By immersing ourselves in positive self-talk and incorporating encouraging messages into our daily routines, we pave the way for a profound transformation within. Each affirmation whispered to ourselves, each quote internalized, becomes a building block in the foundation of our self-belief.

This chapter has highlighted the significance of motivational quotes and affirmations tailored to heal from the wounds of gaslighting. It's a reminder that amidst the shadows of doubt, a powerful tool exists for nurturing our spirits and fortifying our resolve.

As you continue your journey of self-discovery and healing, remember the words that uplift, inspire, and remind you of your innate strength. Let these words be your armor against self-doubt and fuel for resilience, propelling you forward with unwavering determination.

Embrace the transformative power of positive affirmations and motivational quotes, for within their eloquent simplicity lies the key to unlocking your unyielding spirit and reclaiming your fire.

Chapter 13: Creative Healing: Expressive Outlets for Emotional Wellness

"The act of gaslighting does not merely distort one's perception of reality, but seeks to rob them of their truth."

Unknown

When Words and Actions Fail, Let Creativity Speak

In the journey of reclaiming one's self from the clutches of narcissistic manipulation, the road to emotional wellness is often fraught with confusion and pain. The emotional aftermath of gaslighting can leave deep scars, making the path to recovery seem daunting. However, creative healing can offer a powerful means of expression and emotional liberation in these moments of vulnerability. This chapter underscores the therapeutic benefits of diving into creative activities as a method of processing emotions, offering practical strategies that are both accessible and profoundly impactful.

Engaging in creative activities provides a unique outlet for emotional expression that transcends the limitations of conventional communication. For many survivors of gaslighting, putting feelings into words can be an insurmountable challenge. Creative outlets serve as an alternative language that does not rely on words to convey the depth of feeling. Through the act of creation—through painting, writing, music, or any other form of expressive art—individuals can externalize their internal struggles, often leading to insights and emotional breakthroughs that might remain elusive in traditional therapeutic contexts.

The **variety of creative outlets available** means that there is something for everyone, regardless of skill level or artistic inclination. From the simplicity of doodling to the complexity of composing music, these activities do not demand perfection; they instead prioritize expression and the therapeutic process of creation. This chapter explores a wide array of creative options, encouraging readers to experiment and find the medium that resonates most deeply with their personal experiences of healing.

Central to the discussion of creative healing is **embracing creativity as a means to self-discovery and emotional liberation**. In navigating the aftermath of emotional abuse, it is not uncommon for individuals to lose sight of their own identity and voice. Creative endeavors provide a safe space for exploring one's thoughts, emotions, and experiences without judgment. This process not only aids in healing old wounds but also fosters a sense of empowerment and self-awareness that can be transformative.

Moreover, creation is inherently an act of self-care—a declaration of one's worth and reclaiming one's voice. Each brush stroke, word, or note is a step towards reaffirming one's identity and worth beyond the distortion of gaslighting. This chapter emphasizes the power of creativity to heal, rebuild confidence, and strengthen emotional resilience.

The journey of recovery from narcissistic abuse is profoundly personal and can vary significantly from one individual to another. In recognizing this, the strategies presented offer flexibility and adaptability, allowing readers to tailor their creative practice to fit their unique path to emotional wellness. With supportive guidance, readers are encouraged to view creative expression not as an end goal but as an ongoing process of growth and discovery.

Through the lens of creative healing, this chapter sheds light on the potential for art, in its many forms, to catalyze emotional recovery and personal empowerment. It is a testament to the extraordinary capacity of humans to find beauty and strength in the face of adversity, using creativity as both a refuge and a tool for self-reclamation.

Engaging in creative activities can be a powerful tool for exploring and processing emotions, especially in the aftermath of gaslighting. These therapeutic outlets offer a safe and constructive space to express feelings and experiences that may have been invalidated or dismissed. Through journaling, art therapy, or music, creating can help individuals regain a sense of agency and control over their narratives. Emotional healing and growth become possible through creative outlets, nurturing the inner self, and providing a much-needed catharsis.

Journaling, for example, allows individuals to reflect on their experiences, thoughts, and emotions in a private and non-judgmental way. It provides an opportunity to process and make sense of complex emotions and track patterns and progress over time. Writing can serve as a form of release, giving voice to feelings that may have been suppressed or silenced. Additionally, it allows for exploring new perspectives and insights, promoting self-awareness and personal growth.

Art therapy offers another avenue for emotional expression and healing. Through various art forms, such as drawing, painting, or sculpting, individuals can externalize their internal experiences and emotions. Art can visually represent one's journey, allowing for a deeper understanding and acceptance of oneself. It can also be a powerful tool for processing and transforming negative emotions into something positive and cathartic.

Music, too, can be a transformative outlet for emotional wellness. Whether it is through listening to or creating music, the rhythm and melody can evoke and amplify emotions, providing a means for release and validation. Music can connect with our deepest feelings, allowing for a cathartic experience and promoting healing and restoration.

Explore the Therapeutic Benefits of Engaging in Creative Activities for Emotional Processing

Engaging in creative activities can provide numerous therapeutic benefits for emotional processing. By expressing oneself creatively, individuals can:

1. *Validate their emotions:* Creative outlets provide a space where individuals can validate their feelings and experiences without judgment or criticism. Through writing, art, or music, they can voice their pain, anger, and confusion, allowing for validation and validation.

2. *Release pent-up emotions:* Emotional experiences, particularly those associated with gaslighting, can be intense and overwhelming. Engaging in creative activities offers an outlet for releasing pent-up emotions safely and healthily. This release can help individuals find relief and release tension, promoting emotional well-being.

3. *Gain a sense of control:* Gaslighting can leave individuals feeling powerless and out of control. Engaging in creative outlets allows them to regain a sense of agency and control over their own experiences. They can shape their narratives and reclaim power by actively creating and expressing themselves.

4. *Process and make sense of complex emotions:* Creative activities provide a medium for exploring and processing complex emotions. Writing, art, and music allow individuals to delve into their feelings, thoughts, and experiences, helping them make sense of the complexities of their emotions and experiences.

5. *Foster self-reflection and self-awareness:* Engaging in creative activities encourages self-reflection and self-awareness. By giving voice and form to their emotions, individuals can better understand themselves, their feelings, and their experiences. This increased self-awareness can be instrumental in healing and personal growth.

Exploring Expressive Outlets for Emotional Liberation

Engaging in creative activities can be a powerful way to express our feelings and begin the healing process after experiencing gaslighting. The creative process allows us to tap into our inner selves and voice emotions that may have been suppressed or invalidated. When we create, we permit ourselves to be vulnerable and authentic, allowing our true selves to emerge and be seen.

Journaling is a simple and effective way to engage in self-reflection and emotional processing. We can gain clarity and perspective on our experiences by putting our thoughts and feelings onto paper. Journaling allows us to explore our emotions in a safe and private space, free from judgment or gaslighting tactics. It can also help us track patterns and identify triggers, enabling us to understand ourselves and our reactions better.

Art therapy is another powerful tool for emotional healing. Through visual expression, we can communicate complex emotions that may be difficult to put into words. Art can be a cathartic process, allowing us to release pent-up emotions and find solace in creation. Art therapy offers a non-verbal outlet for self-expression and healing, whether painting, drawing, collage, or sculpture.

Music can also play a significant role in our emotional well-being. Listening to music that resonates with our emotions can provide comfort and validation. It can also be a form of self-care, creating a soothing and nurturing environment. Additionally, playing an instrument or singing can be a way to engage in the creative process and express ourselves actively. Music has a unique ability to evoke intense emotions and connect us to our innermost selves.

Dance and movement offer yet another outlet for emotional release and healing. Moving our bodies deliberately and expressively can help us connect with our emotions and release any tension or anxiety we may be holding. Dance can be a form of self-care and a means of reclaiming our bodies after gaslighting has caused us to question our worth and agency.

Exploring nature can also be a therapeutic creative outlet. Spending time outdoors, whether walking in the park or hiking through the woods, can help us reconnect with ourselves and find solace in the beauty of the natural world. Nature has a way of calming and grounding us, allowing us to find peace and clarity amidst the chaos of gaslighting.

Engaging in creative outlets can be a powerful form of self-care and emotional healing. These activities provide us with a means of expressing ourselves authentically and processing our emotions constructively. By nurturing our inner selves through creative expression, we can begin to heal the wounds inflicted by gaslighting and emerge stronger and more resilient.

Our journey of healing and self-discovery continues as we explore the power of creativity as a means to emotional liberation. Engaging in creative activities provides an outlet for constructively expressing emotions and processing experiences. In this final part of our chapter on creative healing, we will delve into how embracing creativity can lead to self-discovery and emotional growth.

When we allow ourselves the freedom to express our innermost thoughts and feelings through creative outlets, we embark on a journey of self-discovery. We gain insights into our true selves through art, writing, music, or any other form of creative expression. These outlets allow us to explore our emotions and experiences safely and nonjudgmentally, enabling us to understand ourselves more deeply.

Moreover, creativity offers a sense of emotional liberation. By giving voice to our emotions, we release pent-up feelings and experiences that may have been stifled or invalidated in the gaslighting dynamic. We can reclaim our feelings through creative expression, embracing them as valid and deserving recognition.

Journaling, for example, allows us to externalize our thoughts and emotions, gaining clarity and perspective on our experiences. Putting pen to paper creates a space where our thoughts and feelings can be seen, acknowledged, and understood. This practice of self-reflection serves as a powerful tool for personal growth, helping us navigate the complexities of our healing journey.

Art therapy is another valuable outlet that taps into our innate creativity to promote emotional well-being. **We can express our emotions nonverbally through various art forms, such as painting, drawing, or sculpture.** Creating art can be cathartic, allowing us to release and transform our pain into something tangible and meaningful.

Music, too, holds the power to heal and uplift our spirits. Whether we play an instrument, sing, or listen to music, it can evoke emotions and solace in times of distress. Music can express what words fail to convey and provide comfort, inspiration, or motivation on our healing journey.

As we embrace creativity as a means to self-discovery and emotional liberation, it is important to remember that there are no right or wrong ways to express ourselves. The beauty of creativity lies in its fluidity and individuality. What matters is that we find outlets that resonate with us and allow us to express ourselves authentically.

Let us continue to explore the diverse world of creative activities, embracing the ones that call to our hearts and souls. Through creativity, we can nurture our inner selves, tapping into our innate resilience and capacity for growth. We empower ourselves to heal, transform, and reclaim our fire by engaging with these expressive outlets.

Embracing Your Creative Journey

As you conclude this chapter, remember the profound impact of engaging in creative activities **on your emotional well-being**. Art, music, writing, and other forms of creative expression are not mere hobbies; they are powerful tools that can help you navigate the complex terrain of healing from emotional wounds. Immersing yourself in these outlets opens doors to self-discovery and resilience.

Your Path to Healing

Self-expression through creativity is a pathway to healing. Allow yourself the time and space to explore the depths of your emotions through art or writing. These outlets offer a sanctuary where your thoughts, feelings, and experiences can be heard. **Through creativity, you can process, release, and transform your pain** into something beautiful and empowering.

Liberation through Creativity

Embrace creativity as a form of liberation. Your inherent creativity is a source of strength and healing. You reclaim power over your narrative and emotions by daring to express yourself. Remember, **you are the author of your story**, and through creative outlets, you can redefine your journey beyond the shadows of doubt.

Take Action:

- **Engage in a creative activity** whenever you feel overwhelmed or stifled by emotions.
- **Start a journal** as a reflective tool to explore your inner world.

- **Create art** as a way to externalize and process your feelings.
- **Experiment with music** to connect with your emotions uniquely.

Embrace these outlets as **more than mere pastimes** but as lifelines to your emotional well-being. You will find solace, growth, and a renewed sense of self in your creative journey. Let your creativity light the way to emotional freedom and empowerment.

Chapter 14: Allies in the Fight: Supporting Others through Gaslighting

"Strength lies in knowing your own truth and not allowing

another's deceit to diminish your self-belief."

Michelle Obama

Gaslighting, a pernicious form of psychological manipulation that sows seeds of doubt in the targeted individual, can leave victims questioning their reality, memories, and sanity. It's a cornerstone tactic of narcissistic manipulation, leading to confusion, isolation, and self-doubt. This pervasive issue demands our understanding and vigilance and beckons us to stand as allies to those trapped in its grip. As we venture deep into strategies for aiding loved ones, it's crucial to recognize that **offering a compassionate hand can be a lifeline for**

someone struggling to break free from the shackles of gaslighting.

Recognizing the signs of gaslighting in someone's life is the first pivotal step. These can range from expressions of self-doubt to apologizing excessively, withdrawing from social interactions, or showing a notable decline in self-esteem. Victims often feel a profound sense of isolation, believing that no one else sees what they're enduring or would even consider them. Here lies our potential to enact real change. **By identifying these red flags**, we become better equipped to offer meaningful support, opening avenues of trust and communication often barricaded by the manipulator.

Offering empathetic support to someone experiencing gaslighting involves more than just being a sympathetic ear; it's about validating their feelings and experiences without immediately jumping to solve their problems. This reinforcement can be the counterweight needed against the disorienting effects of gaslighting. It helps the affected individuals to start trusting their perceptions again, gradually reclaiming their reality. During these interactions, **empathy proves to be your most powerful tool**, forging a path through the deceit sown by their manipulator and helping to rebuild the self-esteem that's been eroded.

Becoming a compassionate ally means also recognizing your boundaries and the limitations of your support. Directing those affected toward professional help when necessary is crucial. It underscores an understanding that the journey to recovery can be complex and fraught with setbacks. **Professional guidance** offers a structured and informed approach that's indispensable. It's about balancing being supportive and advocating for professional intervention when the situation escalates beyond your scope of assistance.

However, the act of supporting someone through gaslighting requires a delicate balance. It's vital to **respect the autonomy of the person you're trying to help**, ensuring they are in control of their healing journey. This respect fosters a safe environment, encouraging them to actively engage with their healing process rather than feeling coerced or further controlled. It's a testament that, while you're walking this path alongside them, it's their journey to reclaim.

This support not only aids the individual but enriches your understanding of narcissistic manipulation, further preparing you to navigate or prevent such dynamics in the future. It's a reciprocal process where **each party learns and grows**, transforming adversity into a profound learning experience.

Lighting the Way Forward

The essence of being an ally in the fight against gaslighting transcends mere support; it's about empowering those affected to recognize abuse, seek help, and ultimately, **reclaim their sense of self-worth**. Through empathy, validation, and respectful guidance towards professional assistance when necessary, we can help illuminate the path out of manipulation's shadow. This collaborative journey not only aids the victim in rebuilding their self-esteem but fortifies our collective resilience against such psychological warfare.

The journey of overcoming and understanding gaslighting, as laid out in this narrative, culminates in recognizing the strength in unity. By standing with those affected, we facilitate their recovery and fortify our communal defenses against such subtle yet devastating control tactics. It's a testament to the power of compassion, understanding, and collective resolve in facing the challenges posed by narcissistic manipulation. Armed with these insights, we step into a world more prepared to shield, support, and empower—**ensuring no one has to navigate the treacherous waters of gaslighting alone.**

Learn How to Recognize Signs of Gaslighting in Others and Offer Empathetic Support

Gaslighting can be an insidious form of manipulation that leaves its victims feeling confused, isolated, and doubting their reality. As a compassionate ally, it is crucial to recognize the signs of gaslighting in others and offer empathetic support. By doing so, you can create a safe space for them to heal, grow, and regain their sense of self-worth.

One key sign of gaslighting is when someone consistently denies or dismisses another person's thoughts, feelings, and experiences. This can leave the victim feeling invalidated as if their reality is being erased. As an ally, it is important to offer validation by affirming their feelings and experiences. Let them know that their emotions are valid and that you believe them. Empathize with their pain and acknowledge their struggles.

Another sign to watch out for is when someone constantly questions another person's memory or perception of events. Gaslighters may twist the truth, distort facts, or even present outright lies to make their victims doubt themselves. As a supportive ally, you can offer reassurance by reminding them of their strengths and affirming their abilities. Help them trust their instincts and encourage them to rely on their judgment.

Gaslighters often employ tactics such as blame-shifting and deflection to avoid taking responsibility for their actions. They may make the victim feel guilty or responsible for their mistreatment. As an ally, it is essential to remind the person experiencing gaslighting that they are not to blame. Please encourage them to set boundaries and hold the gaslighter accountable for their behavior.

Furthermore, gaslighters may engage in attempts to isolate their victims from friends, family, and support systems. They may discourage or undermine relationships, making it harder for the victim to seek help. As an ally, you can provide support by staying connected and available. Offer a listening ear, provide resources and information, and encourage professional help.

Offering empathetic support to someone experiencing gaslighting can make a difference in their healing journey. Your validation, empathy, and understanding can help them regain their confidence and trust in their perceptions and ultimately break free from the manipulation and control of the gaslighter. Remember, they are not alone, and with your support, they can reclaim their sense of self-worth and thrive.

Supporting Those Affected by Gaslighting Through Validation, Empathy, and Practical Solutions

Being a compassionate ally to someone who is experiencing gaslighting is a critical role that can make a significant impact on their journey to healing and reclaiming their sense of self. Your support, validation, and understanding can provide the necessary strength for them to recognize the abuse, seek help, and ultimately break free from manipulation and control. So, how can you be a practical and effective ally to those affected by gaslighting?

First and foremost, validation is key. Gaslighting is a form of psychological abuse that thrives on making the victim doubt their reality. By validating their experiences and emotions, you are helping to counteract the effects of gaslighting. *Reassure them that their feelings are valid and that what they are experiencing is not their fault.* Please encourage them to trust their instincts and rely on their judgment.

Empathy is another vital component of being a compassionate ally. *Try to put yourself in their shoes and imagine how it feels to be constantly manipulated and undermined.* Be present with them in their pain and offer a listening ear. Avoid judgment or invalidating their experiences. Instead, show empathy and permit them to feel anger, sadness, confusion, or whatever emotions they may be experiencing.

In addition to offering emotional support, practical solutions can be incredibly empowering for someone facing gaslighting. *Please educate yourself about gaslighting tactics and share your knowledge with them.* Help them identify the signs of gaslighting, such as constant denial, twisting the truth, and making them question their memory. Please encourage them to keep a journal of instances where they feel manipulated, as this can help them see patterns and gain clarity about the abuse they are experiencing.

Encourage them to set and uphold boundaries, even if the gaslighter tries to undermine or violate those boundaries. *Help them practice assertiveness by role-playing different scenarios.* This can give them the confidence to stand up for themselves and assert their truth. Remind them that they have the right to their thoughts, feelings, and opinions and deserve to be treated with respect and dignity.

However, it is essential to recognize that while your support is crucial, there are limitations to what you can provide. Gaslighting is a form of abuse that requires professional intervention to address and heal fully. Please encourage them to seek help from a therapist or counselor who specializes in trauma and abuse. These professionals can provide the necessary tools and guidance to help navigate the healing process.

Remember, your role as a compassionate ally is to support and empower them, not to fix their problems. *Please encourage them to take ownership of their healing journey and utilize their available resources.* Remind them they are not alone and that there is support and understanding. Offer to accompany them to therapy sessions or help them research local support groups. By doing so, you are giving them the tools and resources they need to reclaim their sense of self-worth and regain control over their lives.

Being a compassionate ally to someone experiencing gaslighting requires empathy, validation, and practical support. You can make a significant difference in their healing journey by offering your understanding, sharing knowledge, and encouraging them to seek professional help. Together, we can create a community of support and empowerment that helps individuals break free from the chains of gaslighting and reclaim their fire.

Understand the Boundaries and Limitations in Offering Support, Emphasizing the Importance of Professional Help

Supporting someone who is experiencing gaslighting can be a challenging task. While your desire to help and provide guidance is commendable, it's crucial to understand the boundaries and limitations in offering support. Gaslighting is a form of emotional abuse that requires specialized knowledge and professional intervention. As a compassionate ally, you can provide emotional support, validate their experiences, and encourage them to seek professional help.

One of the most important aspects of supporting someone through gaslighting is validating their experiences. Gaslighting can make the victim doubt their reality and sanity, so your validation can be compelling. Offer a listening ear and reassure them that their feelings and perceptions are valid. Let them know that they are not alone in their struggles and that you believe them.

Empathy is another crucial element in offering support. Put yourself in their shoes and try to understand their feelings and emotions. Avoid judgment or blame, and instead, offer empathy and understanding. Validate their emotions and let them know that their feelings are normal and valid. Doing so creates a safe and accepting space for them to open up and share their experiences.

While your support is valuable, it's essential to recognize the limitations of your role. Gaslighting is a complex form of emotional abuse, and professional help is often necessary to navigate through it. Please encourage them to seek therapy or counseling from a trained professional who specializes in trauma and abuse. Professional intervention can provide the tools and strategies to help them heal and regain their self-worth.

Respect their autonomy and decision-making process. It's important to remember that, ultimately, they must choose to seek professional help. It's not your responsibility to force or persuade them to do so. Instead, offer gentle encouragement and provide them with information on resources and potential therapy options.

Self-care is paramount, both for you and the person you are supporting. Gaslighting can be emotionally draining for both parties, so ensure you prioritize your well-being. Set boundaries around what you can and cannot do as their support system. Recognize when you need to step back and seek support for yourself. It's important to remember that you cannot save or fix someone else; they hold the power to heal themselves.

Reflecting on Support and Empathy

In navigating the challenging terrain of gaslighting, **recognizing signs of manipulation in others** and extending a compassionate hand of **support** can truly make a difference in someone's journey to healing. Your willingness to **listen, validate, and offer understanding** can be the lifeline that helps them break free from the chains of doubt and confusion.

A Light in the Shadows

You become a sign of hope in their darkest moments by providing practical advice and being there for those affected by gaslighting. Your actions can empower them to **reclaim their self-worth** and stand tall against the tactics of manipulation and control.

Boundaries and Limits: Importance of Professional Help

It's crucial to remember that while your role as an **ally** is significant, there are **boundaries and limitations** to the support you can offer. Encouraging seeking **professional help** when needed is crucial in ensuring a comprehensive and holistic approach to healing.

Reclaiming Your Fire

As you close this chapter on being a supportive ally in the fight against gaslighting, remember that your empathy and understanding can be a powerful force in someone's journey to **reclaiming their sense of self**. Your actions have the potential to ignite a flame of resilience and empowerment in those who have experienced the darkness of manipulation.

Embrace the power of empathy, stand as a pillar of support, and together, let us continue to shine a light on the shadows of doubt, guiding each other toward a brighter, more empowered future.

Conclusion

"Truth is like the sun. You can shut it out for a time,

but it ain't going away."

Elvis Presley

As we draw this exploration to a close, we must acknowledge the journey behind us. We've traversed the shadowy realms of manipulation, confronted the specter of gaslighting, and sought the light of empowerment and healing. This book has guided the turbulent waters of psychological manipulation, offering strategies, insights, and, most importantly, hope to those who have felt its chilling grasp. The path to reclaiming one's reality and sense of self is arduous but deeply rewarding.

Understanding the dynamics of gaslighting and recognizing its signs are the first steps toward liberation. By demystifying this form of manipulation, we equip ourselves with the tools necessary to confront and overcome it. The power of awareness cannot be overstated; the light dispels the shadows of doubt and fear.

Empowerment, however, does not occur in isolation. It unfolds within the mosaic of human relationships and shared experiences. This book has emphasized the importance of a supportive community—friends, family, and allies—who play a crucial role in healing. Their understanding, empathy, and encouragement can be lifelines, pulling those affected by gaslighting back from the brink of despair. Building and maintaining healthy relationships are beneficial and essential for recovery and resilience.

Healing from gaslighting is a deeply personal and, at times, uneven journey. It requires patience, self-compassion, and perseverance. The strategies and insights shared in these pages are starting points tailored to each individual's unique circumstances. Recovery involves setbacks and breakthroughs, each an integral step toward healing. Celebrating small victories and forgiving oneself during moments of struggle are part of this encompassing process.

Professional help is often a crucial element in overcoming complex psychological manipulation. This book has sought to destigmatize the pursuit of mental health support, presenting it as a sign of strength and self-care. Therapists, counselors, and other mental health professionals can offer invaluable guidance, providing a structured environment for healing and growth. Seeking help is a courageous act that can accelerate the journey toward recovery.

The fight against gaslighting—and psychological manipulation more broadly—is ongoing. It extends beyond individual healing, resonating through our relationships, communities, and societies. By fostering awareness and understanding, advocating for mental health, and supporting each other, we can challenge and change the conditions that allow such behaviors to thrive. This book is a chapter in the larger story of our collective movement towards a healthier, more empathetic world.

Epilogue

"Self-trust is the first secret of success.

The essence of heroism."

Ralph Waldo Emerson,

Illuminating the Path Forward

As we bring our journey to a close, it's essential to remember that the road to reclaiming your fire after being engulfed by the shadows of narcissistic manipulation is both challenging and profoundly rewarding. The real-world applications of the concepts and strategies discussed in these pages are numerous and tailored to guide you, step by step, out of the fog of doubt and into the clear light of understanding and self-empowerment.

Empowerment through knowledge and action is at the heart of this transformative journey. We've delved deep into understanding the mechanics of gaslighting, the intricacies of narcissistic manipulation, and the profound impact these experiences can have on one's sense of self and reality. More importantly, we've shared tools and practices for rebuilding self-esteem, setting healthy boundaries, and nurturing respectful relationships that honor your worth.

To apply what you've learned, **start small but think big**. Focus on daily self-reflection, practice boundary-setting in safe environments, and gradually build your capacity for discerning healthy versus unhealthy interactions. Remember, healing is a non-linear process replete with peaks and valleys. Be patient and compassionate with yourself as you navigate through.

While this book aims to provide a comprehensive guide to understanding and overcoming the effects of gaslighting within narcissistic relationships, it is important to **acknowledge the limitations** inherent in any work like this. Each individual's experience is unique, and specific strategies may resonate more with some than others. Therefore, I encourage you to seek further research, connect with professionals, and lean on community resources tailored to your needs.

Taking action based on the insights gained from this book is crucial. Whether reaching out for professional support, engaging in community forums, or implementing the self-care strategies discussed, each step you take is a reaffirmation of your commitment to your well-being and recovery.

As you move forward, remember that you are not walking this path alone. A community of individuals has walked this path before you, and professionals like myself are dedicated to supporting your journey every step of the way.

In closing, let us part with the poignant words of Maya Angelou, a luminary whose wisdom lights the way for many. Her words encapsulate the essence of our journey from darkness into light, from manipulation to empowerment:

"I can be changed by what happens to me. But I refuse to be reduced by it."

May her words remind you of your resilience, strength, and undeniable right to a life filled with respect, dignity, and love. The journey may be long, but it is worth every step.

Bonus Material

Your Questions, Answered!

1. How Can You Recognize the Signs of Gaslighting in a Relationship or Workplace?

Recognizing the early signs of gaslighting is crucial for protecting oneself from harmful impacts. These signs often manifest subtly in personal relationships and the workplace, making them difficult to identify. Initially, the gaslighter may appear charming and attentive, but this behavior typically masks their manipulative intentions. Key early indicators include frequent questioning of your memory or perception (*"Are you sure? You tend to forget things."*), blatant denial of things they've said or done, despite you having clear evidence, and the gradual isolation from your support network, insisting that friends, family, or coworkers are untrustworthy or out to harm you. In the workplace, the gaslighter may take credit for your ideas or blame you for their mistakes. Paying attention to feelings of confusion, self-doubt, and anxiety after interactions with a particular person can also be telling signs. Early recognition of these behaviors as gaslighting is the first step toward seeking help and protecting your mental health and well-being.

2. Are Certain People More Susceptible to Being Gaslighted, and if So, Why?

Specific individuals may be more susceptible to gaslighting due to factors affecting their self-perception and relationship dynamics. Individuals with a history of psychological abuse, low self-esteem, or those who are naturally more trusting and empathetic may find themselves at higher risk. Such individuals might overlook or rationalize early signs of gaslighting due to their desire to see the best in others, fear of confrontation, or place the gaslighter's needs and perceptions above their own. Additionally, people conditioned to doubt their self-worth or capabilities are more likely to accept the gaslighter's manipulations as truth. In professional settings, those new to the workplace or in lower power positions might be more vulnerable, as they are often less likely to challenge authority figures or speak out against unfair treatment for fear of repercussions. Understanding these vulnerabilities is crucial in developing strategies to protect oneself and others from gaslighting.

3. Can Gaslighting Occur Within Families, and How Does It Differ From Other Relationships?

Gaslighting can indeed occur within families, where it often takes on a particularly insidious form due to the inherent trust and authority dynamics. In these relationships, the manipulator might be a parent, sibling, or another close relative, leveraging their position and your emotional bonds to question your memory, perception, and sanity. The effects can be profoundly damaging over time, contributing to long-term psychological distress. Unlike in romantic or professional relationships, family-based gaslighting is complicated by the permanence of familial ties and a more profound sense of obligation, making it harder for individuals to set boundaries or remove themselves from the manipulative environment. The shared history and emotional investment in family relationships also mean that the gaslighter has extensive knowledge of and access to the personal vulnerabilities and insecurities of their target, which they can exploit to maintain control. Recognizing and addressing gaslighting within families requires a nuanced understanding of these dynamics and a compassionate approach that supports healing and resilience for the victim.

4. What Are the Long-Term Psychological Effects of Gaslighting if It's Not Addressed?

If gaslighting is not addressed, it can lead to long-term psychological effects that profoundly impact an individual's mental health and perception of reality. Victims may suffer from chronic self-doubt, severe anxiety, and depression as they continually question their thoughts, memories, and decisions. The erosion of self-esteem is joint, leaving individuals feeling unworthy and incapable. Long-term exposure to gaslighting can also lead to complex post-traumatic stress disorder (C-PTSD), characterized by prolonged periods of emotional numbness, detachment from relationships, and difficulty trusting others. Additionally, individuals may develop an exaggerated sense of fear towards making decisions or asserting themselves, fearing repercussions similar to those experienced during gaslighting episodes. Without intervention, these effects can alter the victim's life trajectory, affecting relationships, careers, and the ability to engage in society confidently and healthily. Recognizing and addressing gaslighting early is crucial to preventing these potentially devastating long-term effects.

5. How Can Someone Differentiate Between Gaslighting and Normal Disagreements in a Relationship?

Differentiating between gaslighting and normal disagreements is vital for maintaining healthy communication and trust between partners. Normal disagreements are a part of any relationship, characterized by an exchange of differing opinions or feelings, where both parties feel heard and respected. These disagreements typically resolve through mutual understanding, compromise, or agreeing to disagree without lingering resentment. On the other hand, gaslighting involves a deliberate attempt to manipulate or undermine one's perception of reality, leading to confusion and self-doubt. It includes tactics such as denying events or conversations that happened, trivializing your feelings or concerns, or shifting blame to make you feel at fault for your actions. When distinguishing between the two, pay attention to behavior patterns over time. If disagreements leave you consistently questioning your memory, feelings, or sanity, or a persistent imbalance of power and respect in the communication, it may indicate gaslighting rather than healthy conflict.

6. What Steps Can You Take to Protect Yourself From Gaslighting in a Digital Context, Such as Social Media?

Protecting yourself from gaslighting in digital contexts, like social media, involves setting boundaries, critically evaluating interactions, and fostering a supportive network. First, limit your exposure by customizing your privacy settings to control who can contact and comment on your posts. Engage critically with the information and interactions you encounter online; not everything you read or see is accurate or well-intentioned. Recognize manipulative tactics often used in digital spaces, such as trolling or spreading misinformation to undermine your confidence or beliefs. Cultivate a supportive online community that respects diverse perspectives and encourages constructive dialogue. Consult with trusted friends or professionals to validate your experiences and feelings when in doubt. Lastly, taking regular breaks from social media can help maintain a healthy perspective and reduce the impact of negative interactions.

7. Are There Specific Strategies for Confronting a Person Who is Gaslighting You?

Confronting someone who is gaslighting you requires a careful and strategic approach, ideally aimed at preserving your mental health and safety. The first step is to trust your perception of reality; keeping a journal or records of interactions can help validate your experiences. Establish clear boundaries with the gaslighter, expressing directly and calmly what behavior is unacceptable and how you expect to be treated. Engaging in these conversations without expecting the gaslighter to acknowledge their wrongdoing is essential, as their primary goal has been to distort your reality to maintain control. Building a support system of friends, family, or professionals who understand the situation can provide emotional support and perspective.

In some cases, particularly where the gaslighting behavior does not change or is accompanied by other forms of abuse, it may be necessary to limit or end contact with the gaslighter. Seeking professional counseling can also be beneficial in healing from the effects of gaslighting and developing strategies to protect oneself in future interactions. Confronting gaslighting is challenging, but taking steps to protect your mental health is paramount.

8. How Does the Recovery Process Differ Between Someone Who Has Been Gaslighted for a Short Time Versus Someone Enduring It for Years?

The recovery process for individuals who have been gaslighted can significantly differ based on the duration of exposure to this form of manipulation. For those who have experienced gaslighting for a short period, recovery might involve re-establishing trust in their perceptions and rebuilding self-esteem, which, although challenging, can be relatively more straightforward with the support of a strong, affirming social network and, if necessary, professional guidance. Short-term victims might also find it easier to separate manipulative behaviors from their self-image and regain confidence in their decision-making abilities more quickly.

Conversely, for individuals who have endured gaslighting over several years, the path to recovery can be more complex and lengthy. The prolonged exposure to manipulation can deeply embed feelings of doubt, fear, and worthlessness, making it harder to trust one's judgment or rebuild self-esteem. These individuals may require extensive therapy to unravel the layers of emotional and psychological damage, addressing any co-occurring mental health issues such as anxiety, depression, or C-PTSD that have developed as a result. The long-term process often includes relearning how to establish and maintain healthy boundaries, deciphering one's thoughts and feelings from the gaslighter's imposed reality, and, crucially, rekindling a sense of self-worth detached from the abuser's influence. Recovery for long-term victims is not only about healing from past manipulation but also involves a significant transformation of one's identity and worldview, necessitating patience, compassion, and comprehensive support.

9. Can Gaslighting Leave Physical Effects on the Body, Alongside Psychological Ones?

While the primary impact of gaslighting is psychological, manifesting in confusion, anxiety, depression, and loss of self-esteem, it can also precipitate physical symptoms due to the stress it induces. Chronic exposure to such psychological stress may result in physical manifestations like headaches, muscle tension, fatigue, and stomach issues. Additionally, stress impacts the immune system, potentially leading to a higher susceptibility to infections and a slower recovery process from illness. Sleep disturbances, such as insomnia or oversleeping, are common among those experiencing intense stress, further exacerbating physical health problems. It's critical to recognize these physical symptoms as potentially linked to psychological stressors, including gaslighting, and address them holistically as part of the recovery process.

10.   What Role Does Cultural Background Play in the Perception and Impact of Gaslighting?

Cultural background significantly influences the perception and impact of gaslighting due to variations in societal norms, values, and communication styles. In cultures with a high value placed on hierarchical relationships and respect for authority, individuals may be more susceptible to gaslighting by figures of authority or elderly family members, as questioning or confronting them might be socially discouraged. Similarly, communities that prioritize collective well-being over the individual might overlook or misinterpret the signs of gaslighting, attributing them to personal shortcomings or necessary sacrifices for the group's harmony. Conversely, in cultures that emphasize individualism and direct communication, victims of gaslighting may more readily identify and confront the behavior, though they might still struggle with the psychological effects. Furthermore, the stigma surrounding mental health issues in certain cultures can prevent individuals from seeking help, complicating the recognition and addressing of gaslighting's impact. Thus, understanding the role of cultural background is crucial in addressing and supporting victims of gaslighting, necessitating culturally sensitive approaches in both personal and professional contexts.

11.   How Can Allies Effectively Support Someone They Suspect is Being Gaslighted Without Overstepping Boundaries?

Allies can play a crucial role in supporting someone they suspect is being gaslighted by maintaining a delicate balance between offering support and respecting the individual's autonomy. Firstly, providing a safe, non-judgmental space for individuals to express their feelings and experiences is essential. Listening attentively and validating their emotions can be immensely empowering, as it contrasts with the gaslighter's intent to undermine their sense of reality. Secondly, rather than directly confronting the gaslighter or insisting on specific actions, allies should focus on empowering the individual. This can be achieved by gently encouraging them to trust their instincts, supporting them in seeking professional help if needed, and providing them with resources about gaslighting and mental health. It's also vital to respect their pace and decisions, even if their process of gaining clarity or taking action is gradual. Finally, consistently reminding them of their strengths and worth can help rebuild the self-esteem that gaslighting often erodes. By adopting these supportive approaches, allies can assist someone experiencing gaslighting in navigating their journey toward recovery without overstepping boundaries or inadvertently diminishing the individual's agency.

12.   What Are the Societal Impacts of Widespread Gaslighting Behaviors, for Example, in Media or Politics?

Widespread gaslighting behaviors, especially in media or politics, can have profound societal impacts, eroding public trust and contributing to a divisive and contentious environment. When leaders or influential figures engage in gaslighting, it can distort public perception of reality, making it challenging for individuals to discern truth from falsehood. This manipulation can lead to confusion, cynicism, and disillusionment among the populace, undermining confidence in authoritative sources and institutions. Furthermore, normalizing such tactics can encourage similar behaviors in interpersonal relationships and workplaces, fostering a culture where manipulation and deceit are tolerated or rewarded. The societal fabric becomes frayed as collective values shift towards skepticism and antagonism, weakening the bonds of community and cooperation. Addressing and mitigating the impact of gaslighting on a societal level thus requires concerted efforts to promote transparency, accountability, and respectful discourse, along with fostering critical thinking skills that empower individuals to question and analyze the information presented to them.

13.   How Do Recommendations for Professional Help Differ Based on the Severity of the Gaslighting Experienced?

The recommendations for professional help in cases of gaslighting vary significantly based on the severity of the experience. For individuals facing mild forms of gaslighting, engaging with a therapist or counselor who specializes in cognitive-behavioral therapy (CBT) can be effective in helping them recognize gaslighting tactics, rebuild confidence, and develop strategies to counteract the manipulation. In moderate cases, where gaslighting has led to more considerable psychological distress or has begun to affect the individual's daily functioning, a multifaceted approach might be necessary. This could include more intensive therapy sessions, possibly integrating elements of trauma-focused therapy, support groups, and, if appropriate, medical intervention to manage symptoms of anxiety or depression in severe cases where gaslighting has resulted in significant mental health issues, long-term psychological treatment might be required. This could encompass prolonged therapeutic engagement with professionals trained in dealing with complex PTSD, potential inpatient care for those experiencing acute mental health crises, and a coordinated care approach to address any concurrent issues such as substance abuse or severe depression. Across all levels, the emphasis is on personalized care that respects the individual's experiences and aims to empower them toward recovery and resilience.

14.   How Can Organizations and Institutions Better Equip Themselves to Recognize and Address Gaslighting Among Their Members or Employees?

Organizations and institutions can better equip themselves to recognize and address gaslighting among their members or employees by implementing comprehensive education and training programs focused on psychological safety and respectful workplace practices. These programs should aim to raise awareness about gaslighting and how it manifests and teach staff to identify signs of such behavior among colleagues and within hierarchical relationships. Additionally, creating clear, accessible avenues for reporting suspicions of gaslighting without fear of retaliation is crucial. This involves establishing robust support systems and clear protocols for investigation that respect the confidentiality and autonomy of those coming forward. Equally important is promoting a culture of empathy and accountability, where manipulative behaviors are neither tolerated nor ignored. By fostering an environment that prioritizes mental health and ethical interactions, organizations can mitigate the damaging effects of gaslighting and support the well-being of their entire workforce.

15.   What Future Research is Needed to Understand Gaslighting and Develop More Effective Interventions Fully?

Future research into gaslighting requires a multifaceted approach to deepen our understanding of this complex phenomenon and develop more effective interventions. Firstly, longitudinal studies that trace the progression and long-term effects of gaslighting in various contexts (e.g., interpersonal relationships, workplaces, and broader societal settings) are necessary. Such research could illuminate the mechanisms through which gaslighting exacerbates or contributes to mental health issues, providing insights into timing and modes of intervention. Secondly, comparative studies across different cultures and socio-demographic groups could reveal how diverse environments and societal norms influence the prevalence, perception, and impact of gaslighting, guiding culturally sensitive interventions. Thirdly, there's a pressing need for research into the effectiveness of various therapeutic approaches for both victims and perpetrators of gaslighting to identify best practices and potentially develop targeted therapies.

Additionally, developing and validating diagnostic tools and assessment measures specific to gaslighting experiences could facilitate early detection and intervention. Finally, exploring technology's role in perpetuating and combating gaslighting could uncover new avenues for prevention and support.

Addressing these gaps in the research landscape will be crucial for devising comprehensive strategies to mitigate the harms of gaslighting and foster resilience among those affected.

THANK YOU

Thank you for investing your time in reading this book. Your willingness to engage with such important topics reflects a profound commitment to personal growth and the health of your professional and personal relationships.

We hope the insights and strategies shared here equip you with the tools to recognize and address gaslighting, fostering environments of respect and understanding. May this knowledge empower you to advocate for yourself and others, contributing to a more compassionate and accountable society.

Your journey towards resilience and empowerment is commendable, and we are grateful to be a part of it.